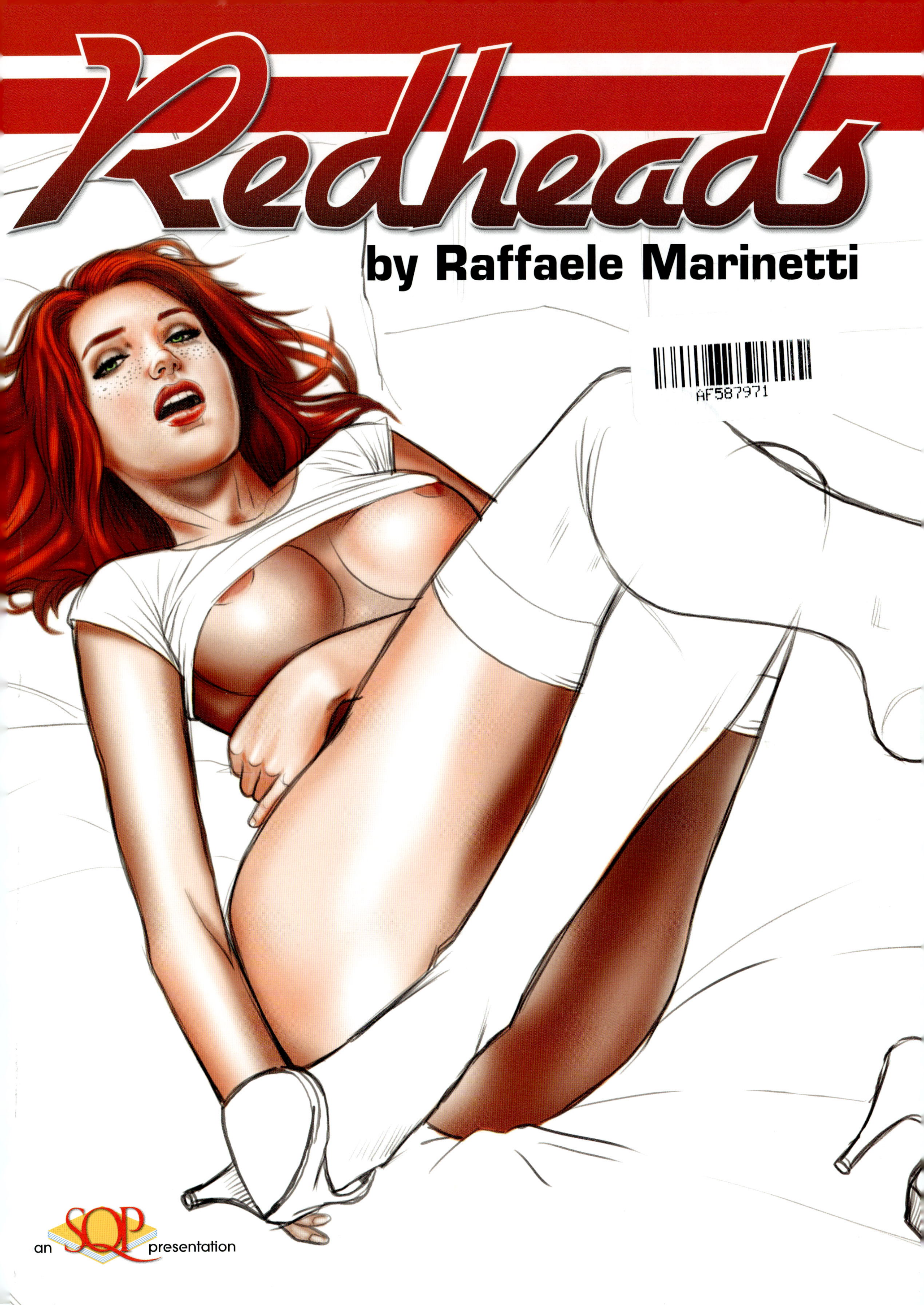

Redheads
by Raffaele Marinetti
AF587971
an SQP presentation

SEEING RED

The Joy of Gingers!

Long celebrated (and often respectfully feared) for their firey nature, redheads are the spice in the genetic stew we all share here on planet Earth. Your blondes and brunettes are standard issue delights, but the redhead stands out in a crowd - her crimson halo of hair a challenge to the brave of heart - "Proceed with caution...but proceed." We love these rare and rambunctious ladies, as does artist Raffaele Marinetti, illustrator and pinuip artist based in Naples, Italy. His fascination with red-heads inspired us to create this mag-nificent collection of digital cuties. Can you handle the heat? Blisters were never this worthwhile!

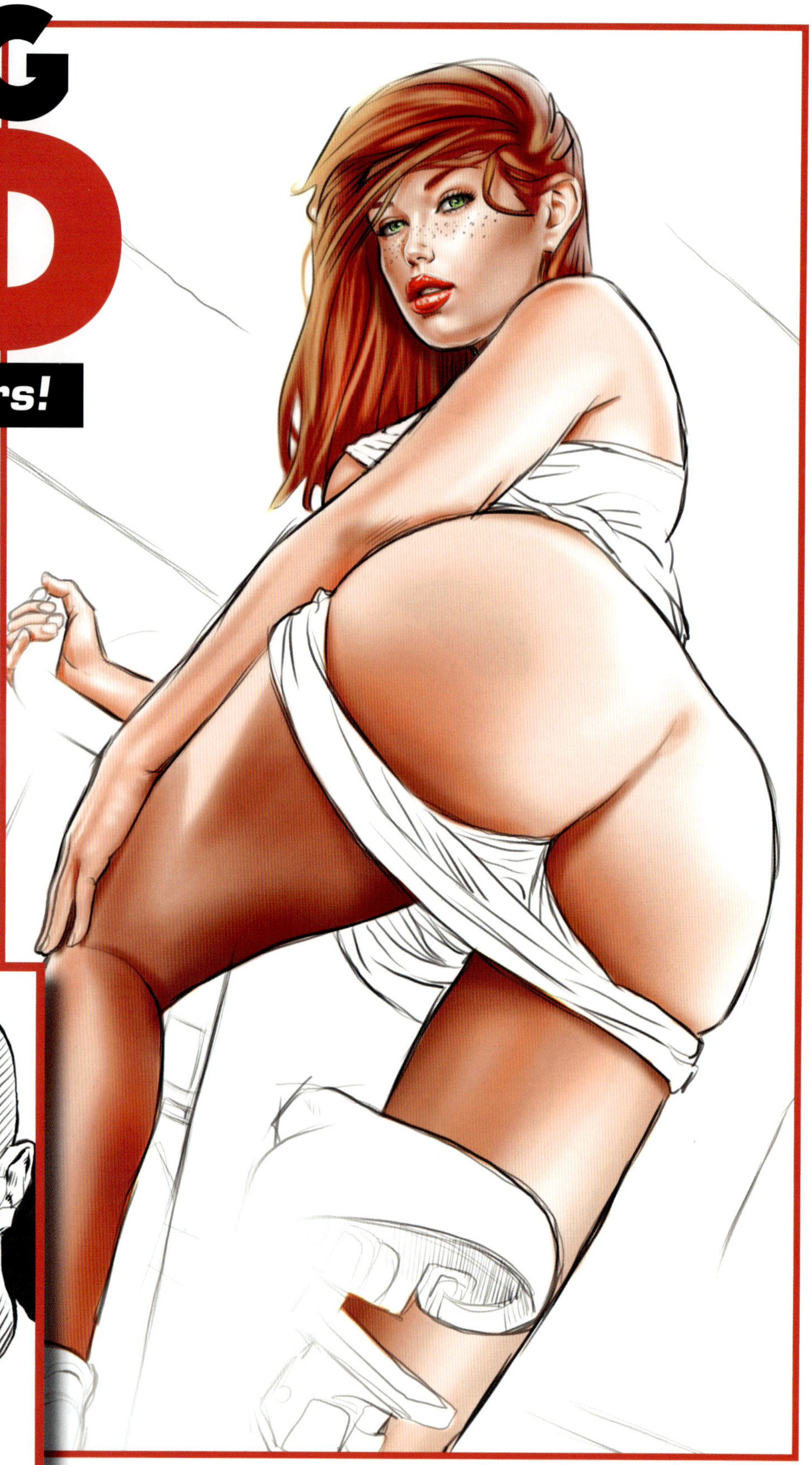

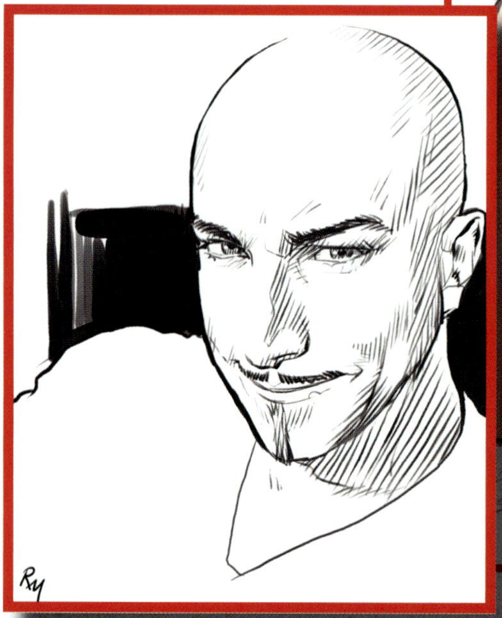

Redheads - by Raffaele Marinetti

All artwork is copyright © 2017 Raffaele Marinetti.
Redheads by Raffaele Marinetti is copyright © 2017 S.Q. Productions Inc.
All rights reserved. Printed in Hong Kong.
Book design by Grassy Knoll Studios.

Published by SQP Inc. - PO Box 248 - Columbus NJ 08022

Sal Quartuccio & Bob Keenan - Publishers

For a free, full color catalog showcasing the entire SQP line of erotic, fantasy, and pin-up artwork, go to: **www.sqpartbooks.com**

Since 1973, showcasing the very finest in fantasy, erotic, & pin-up illustration.

www.sqpartbooks.com

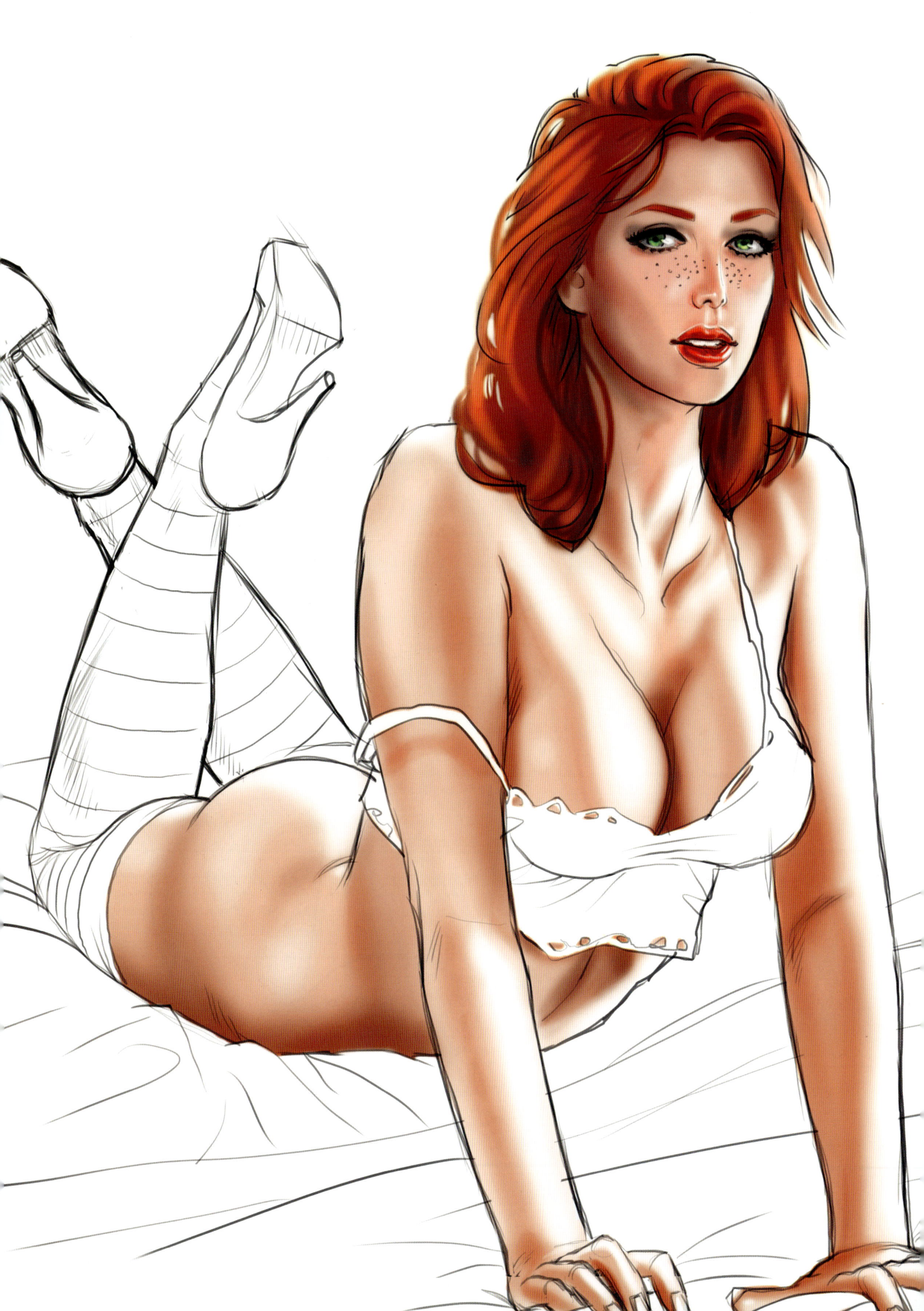

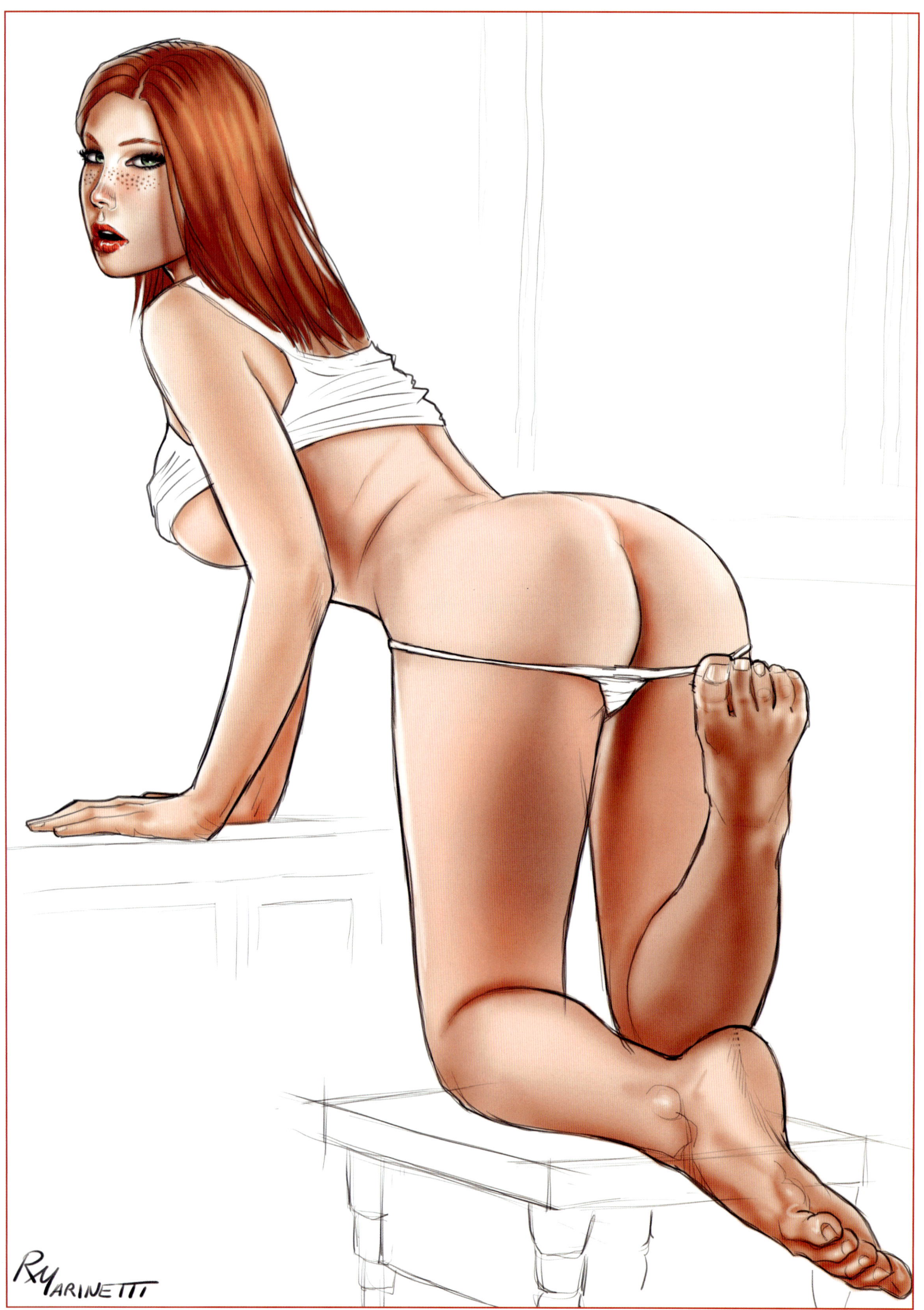

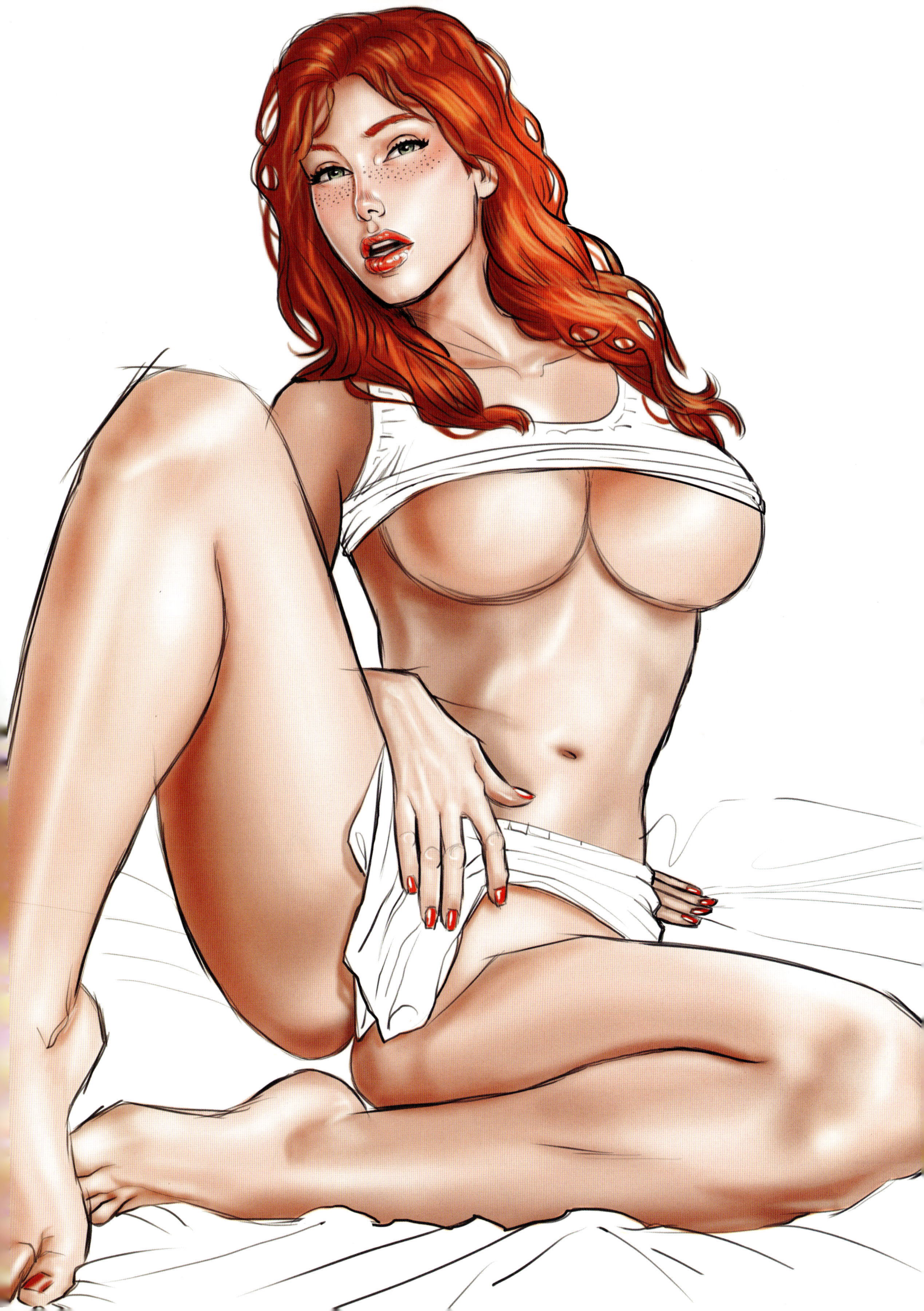

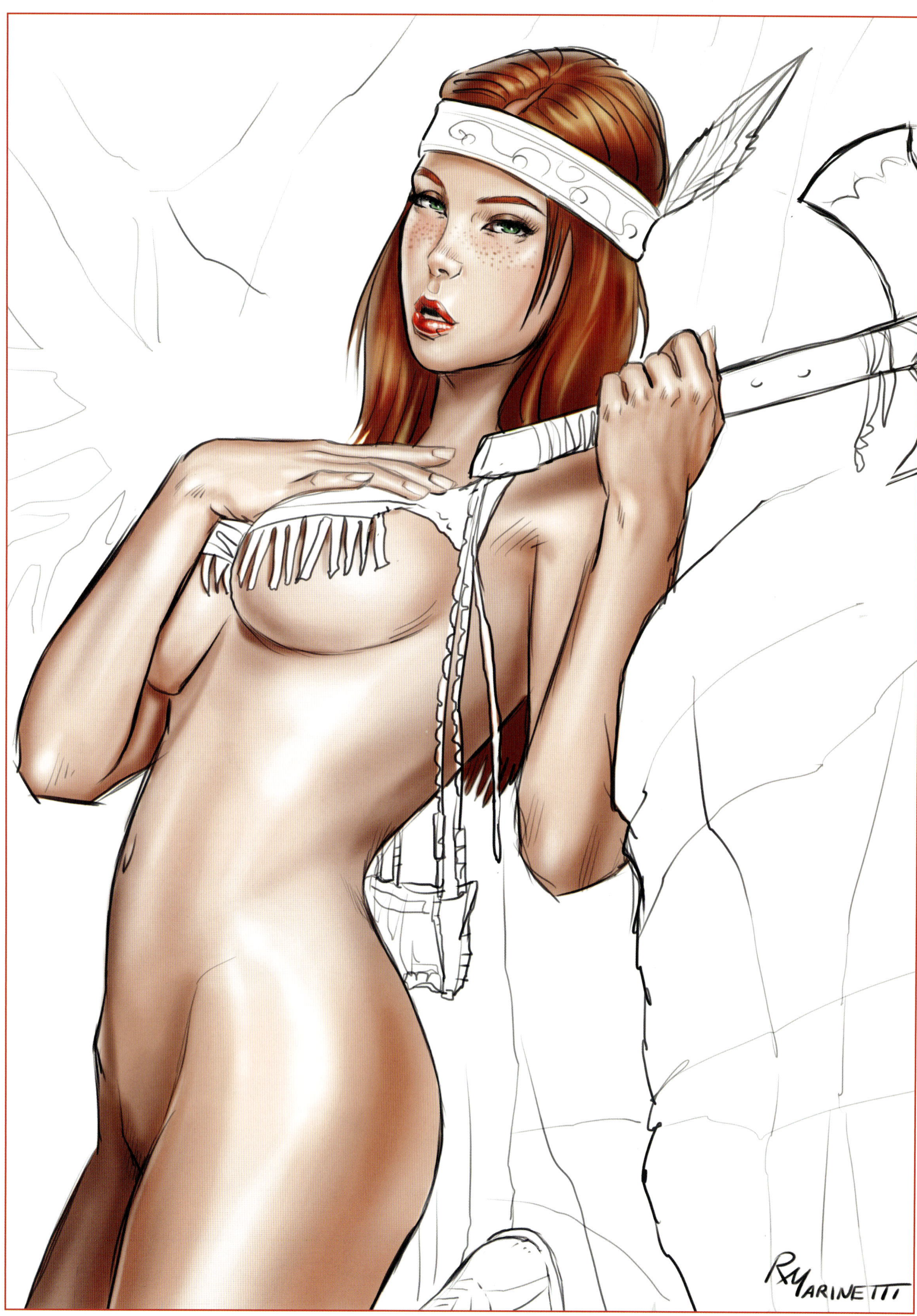

RMARINETTI

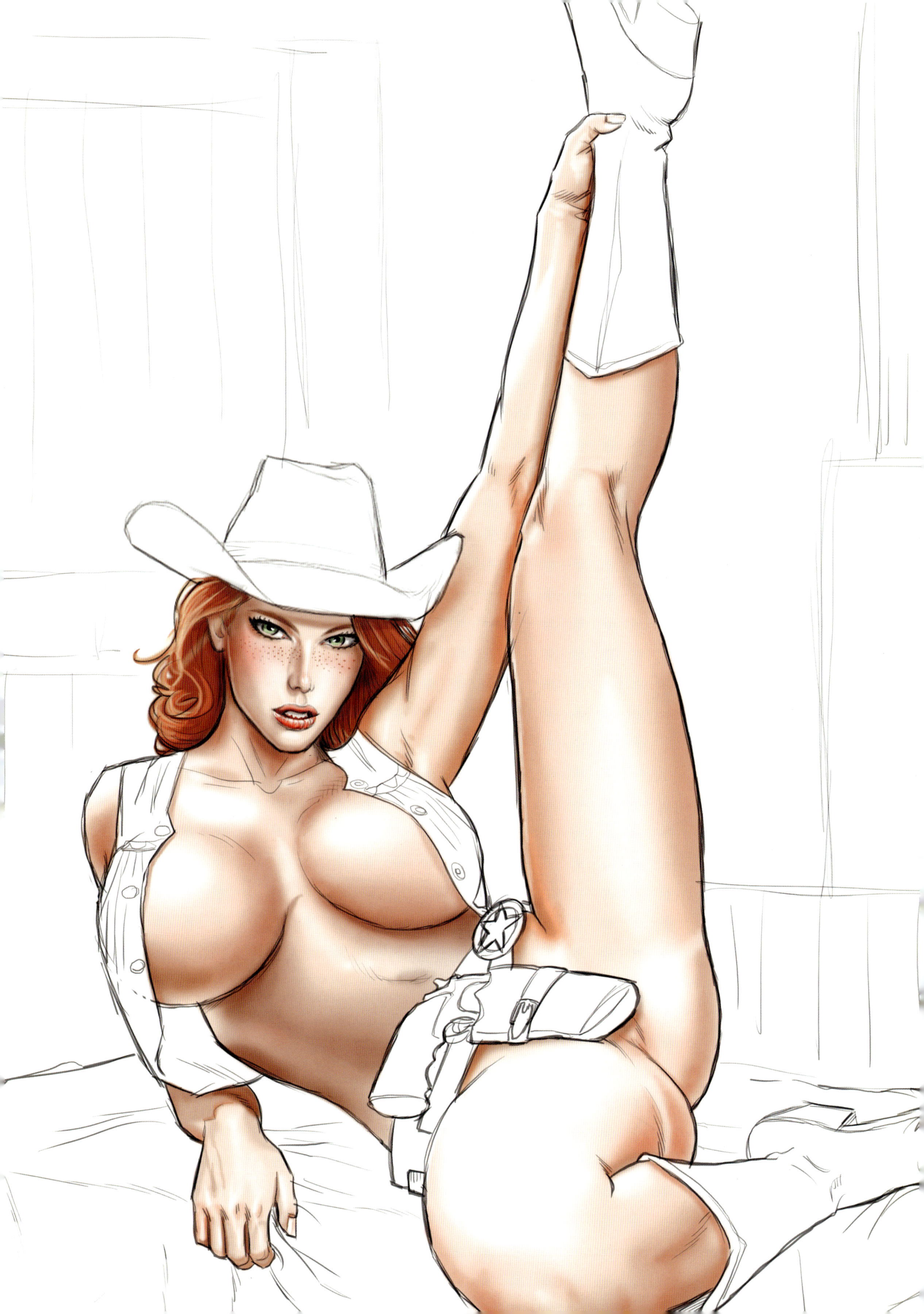

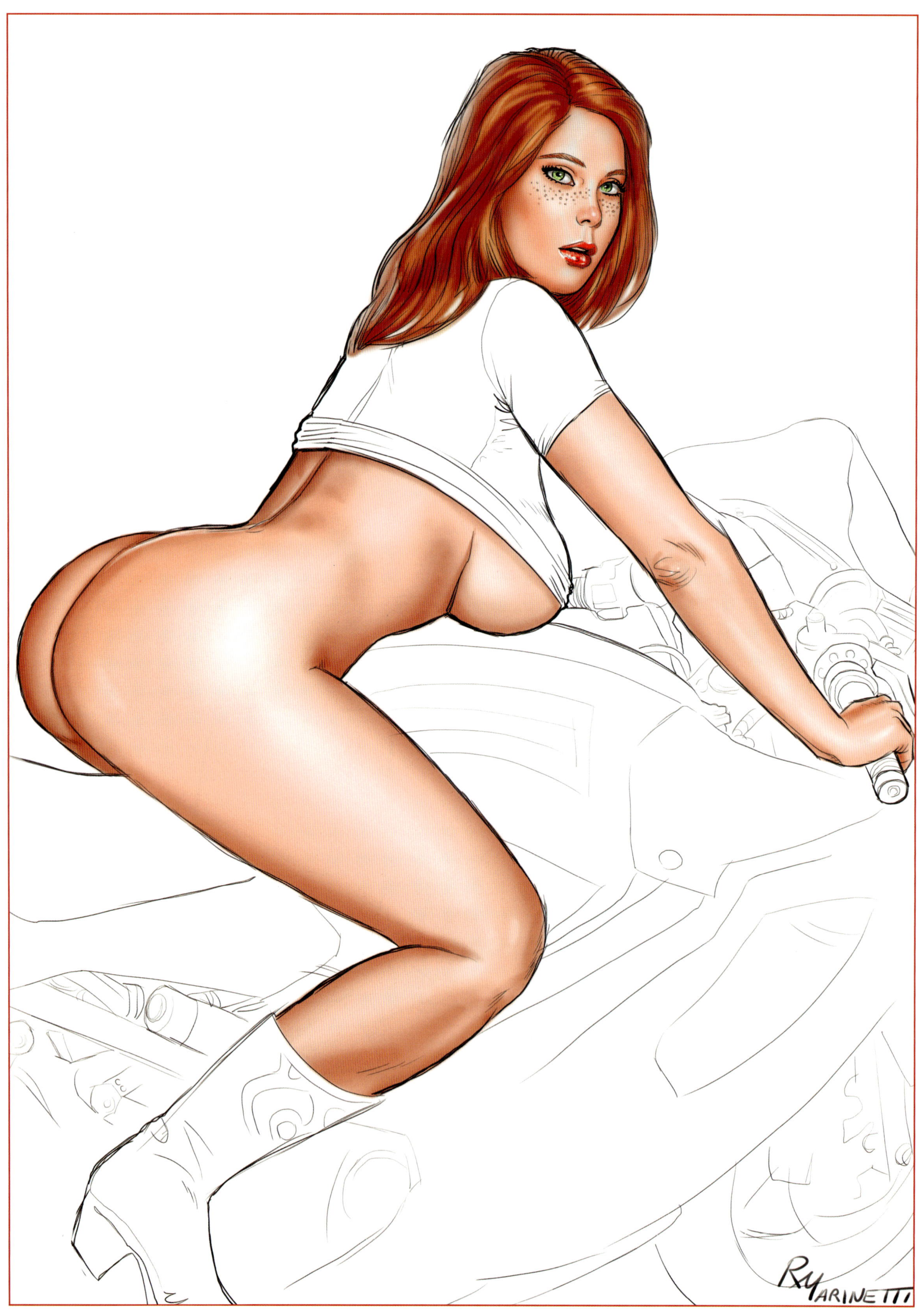

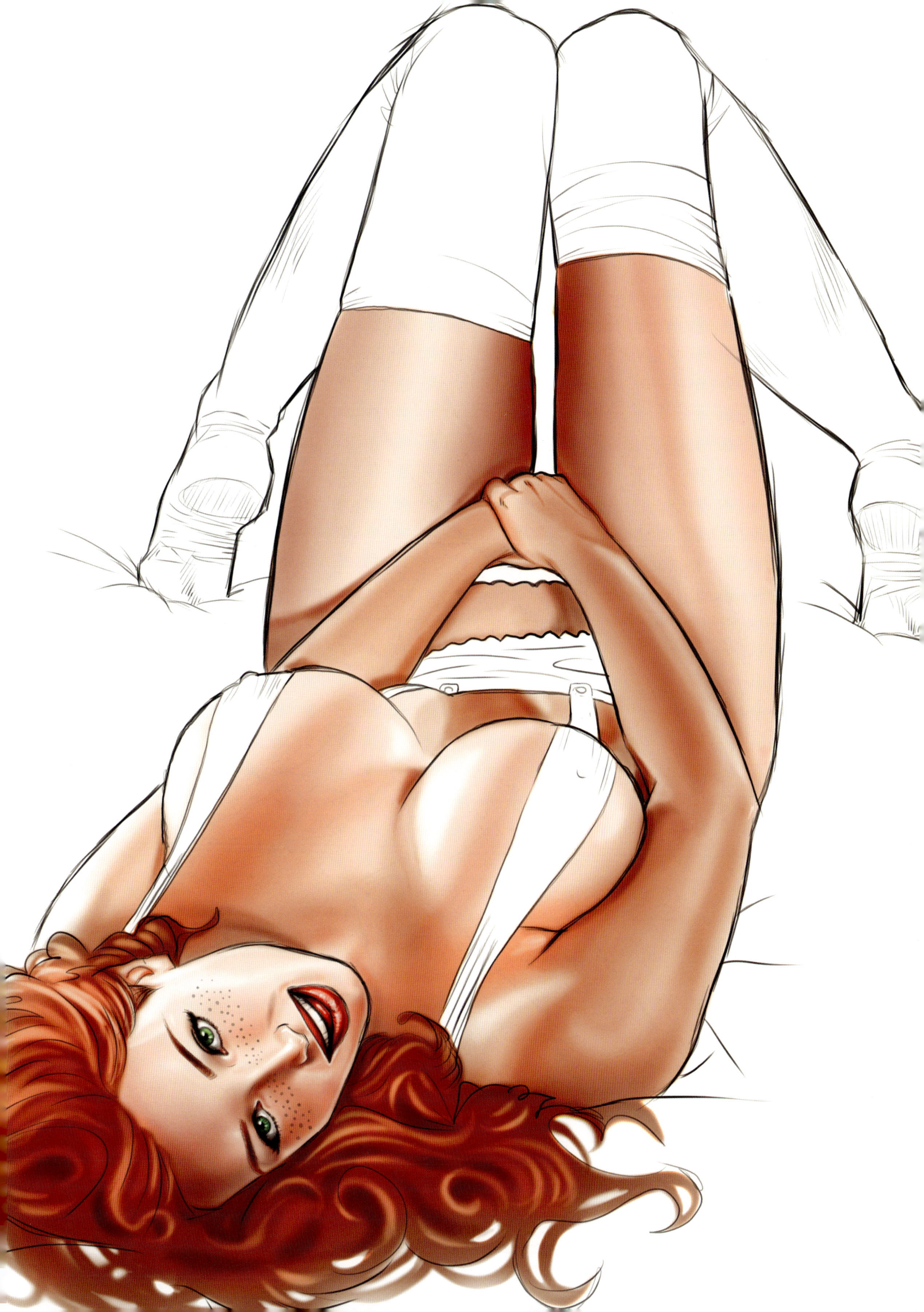

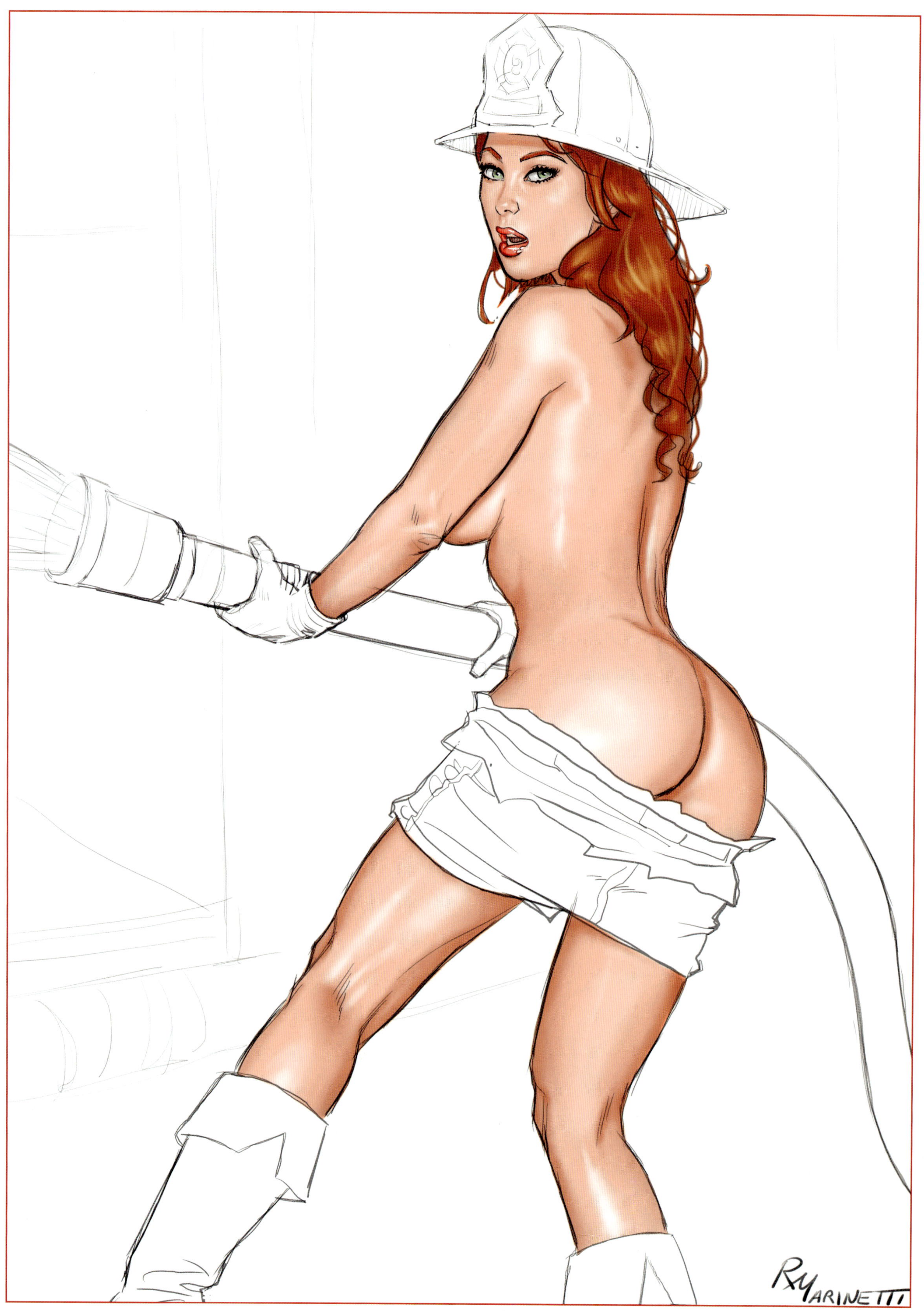
RMARINETTI

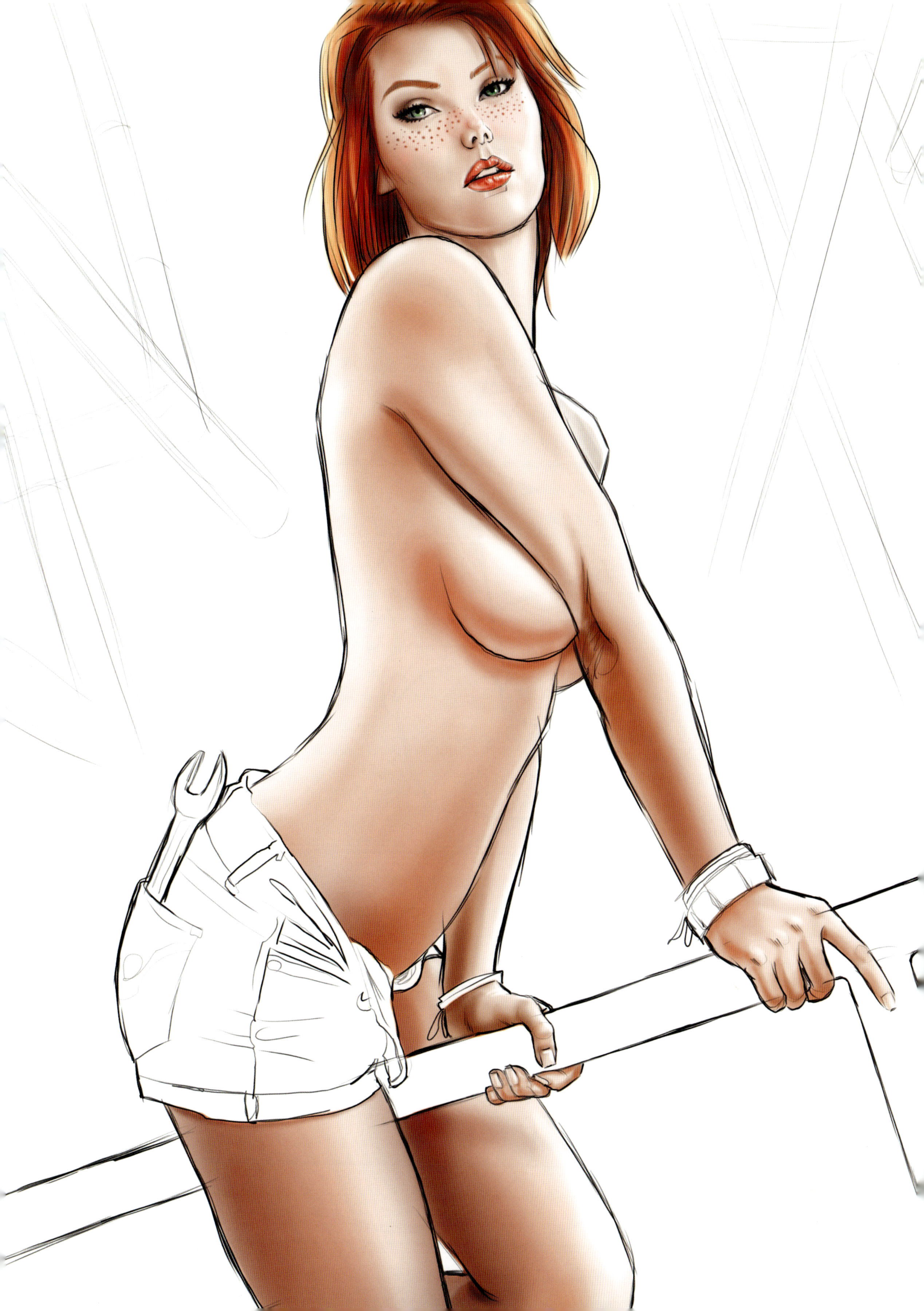

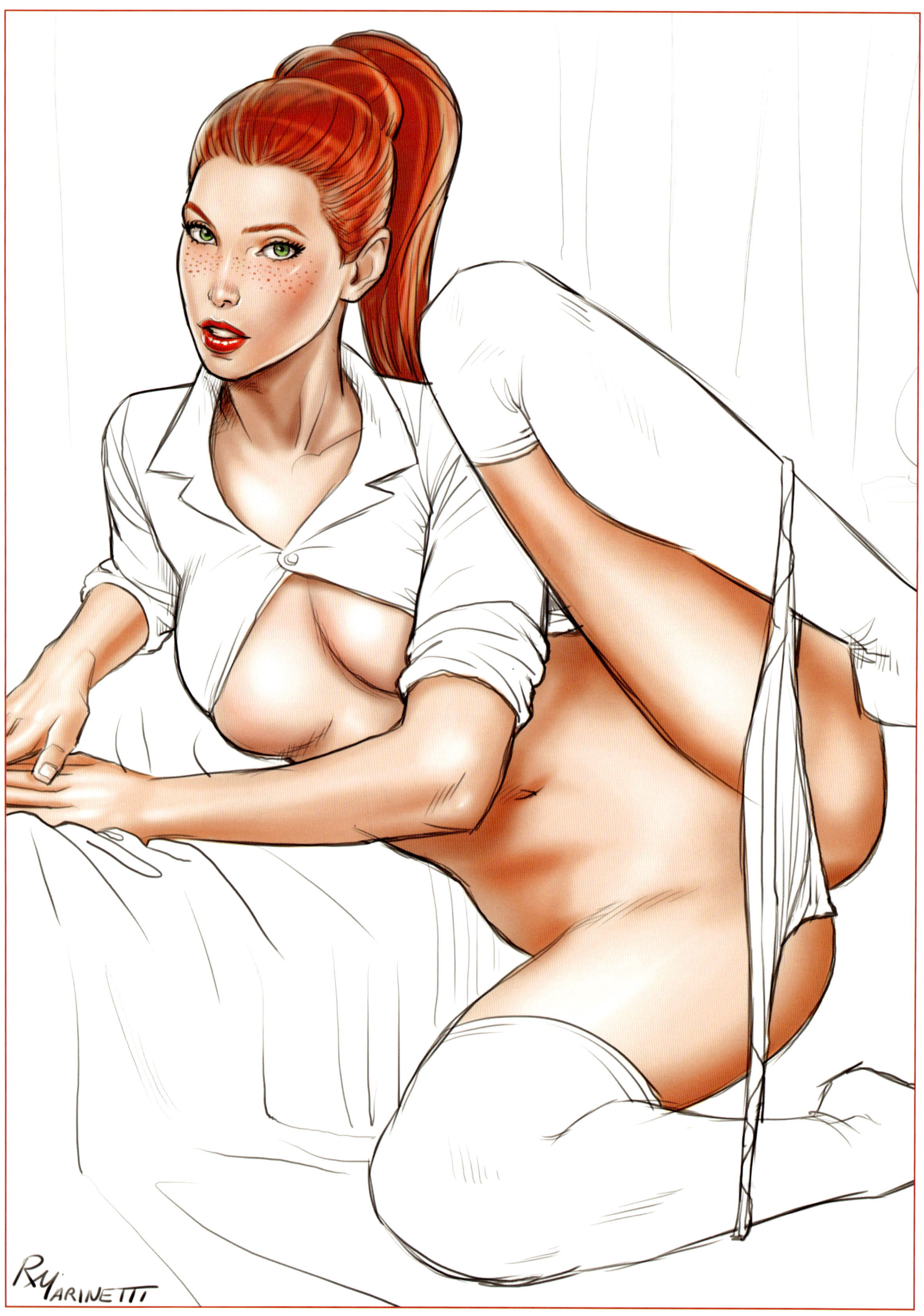

RM MARINETTI

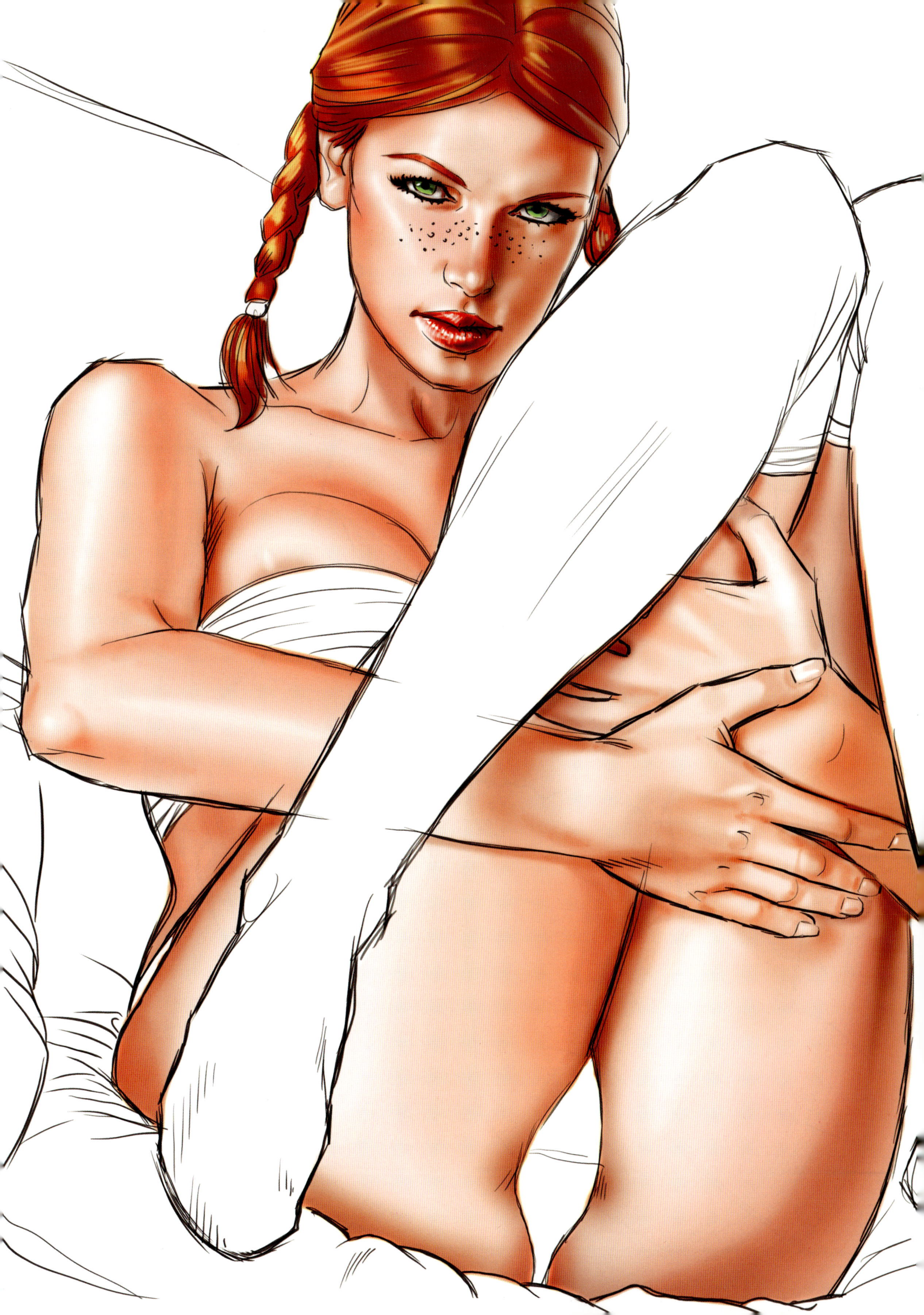

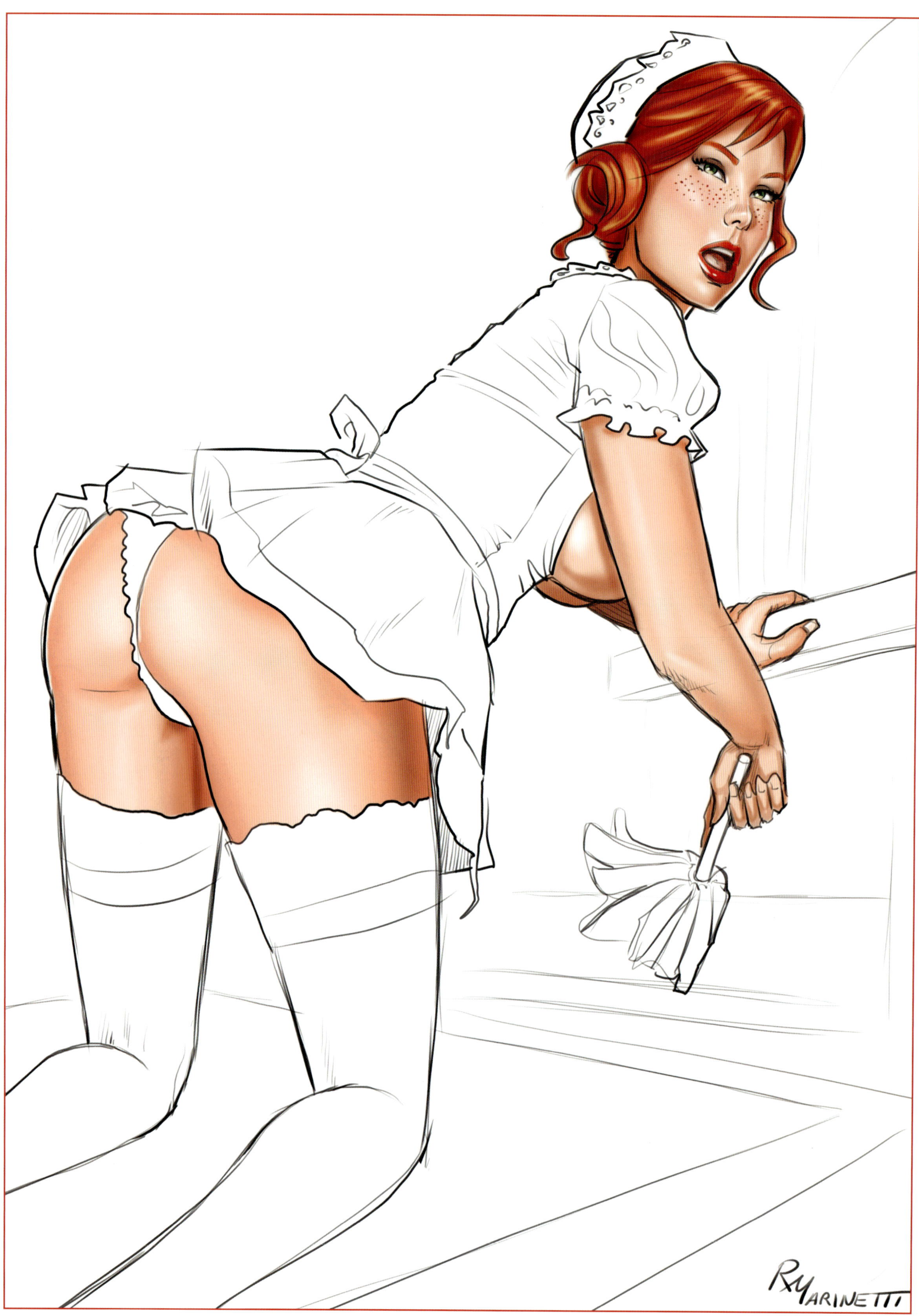
RMARINETTI

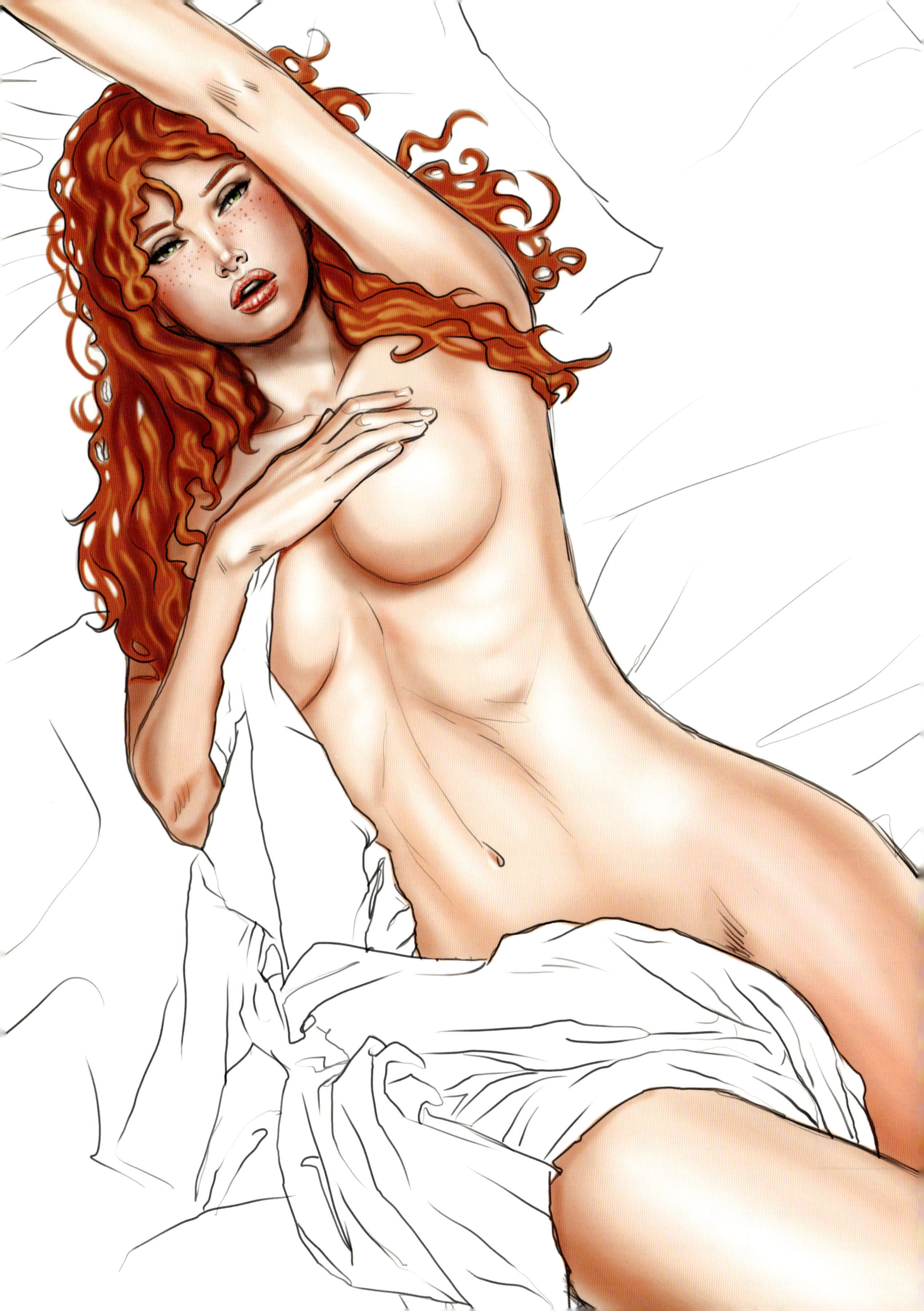

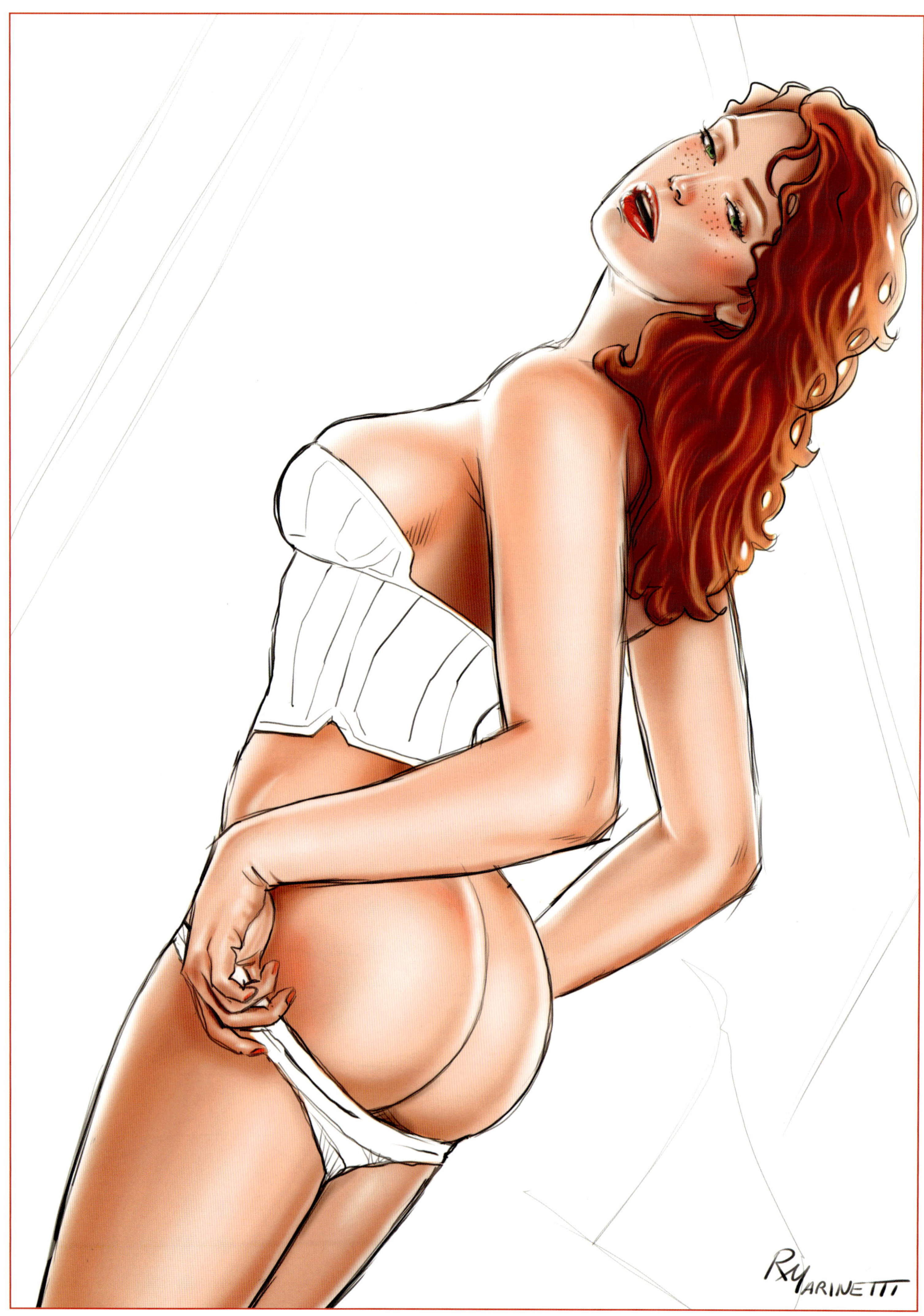
RxMARINETTI

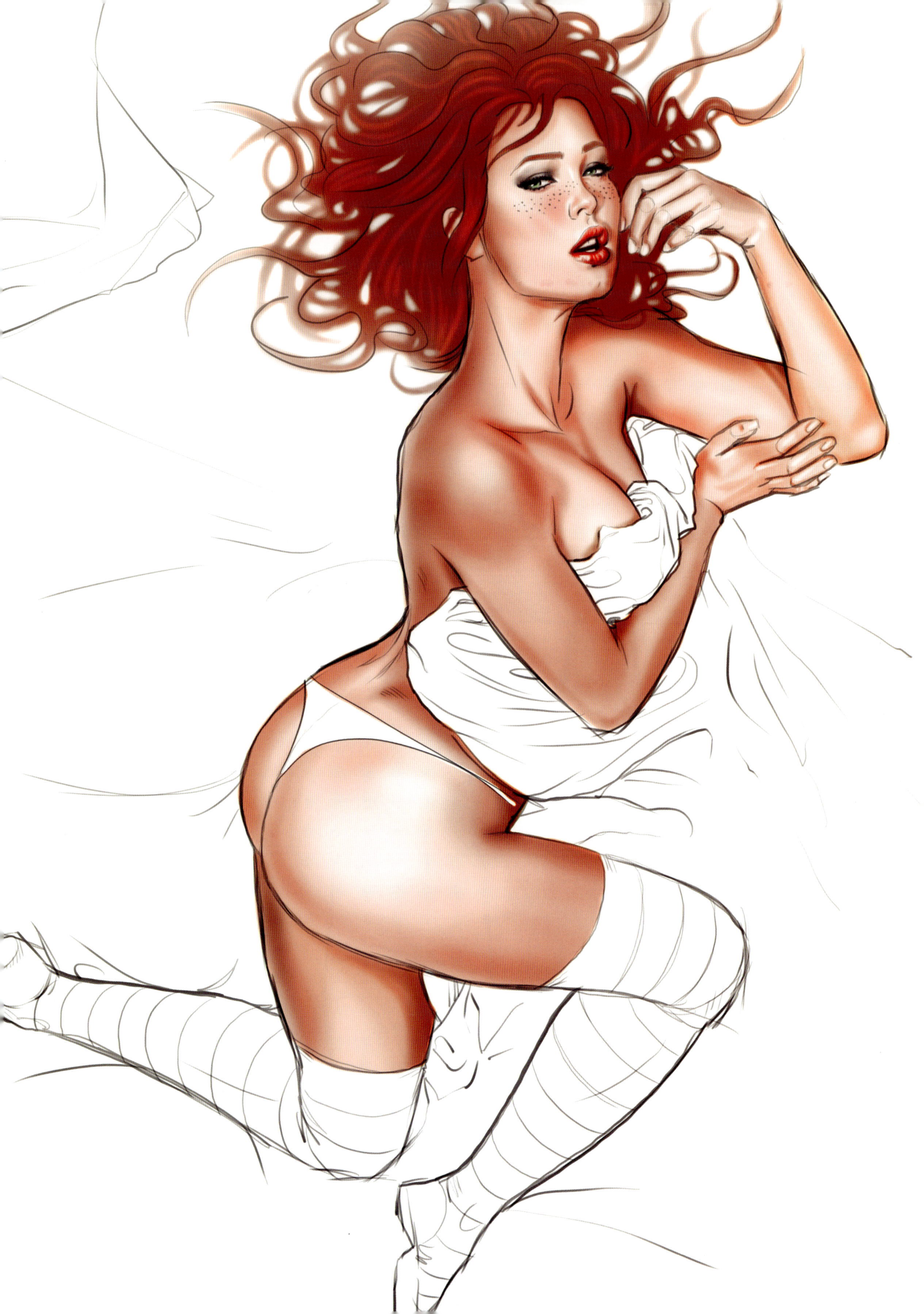

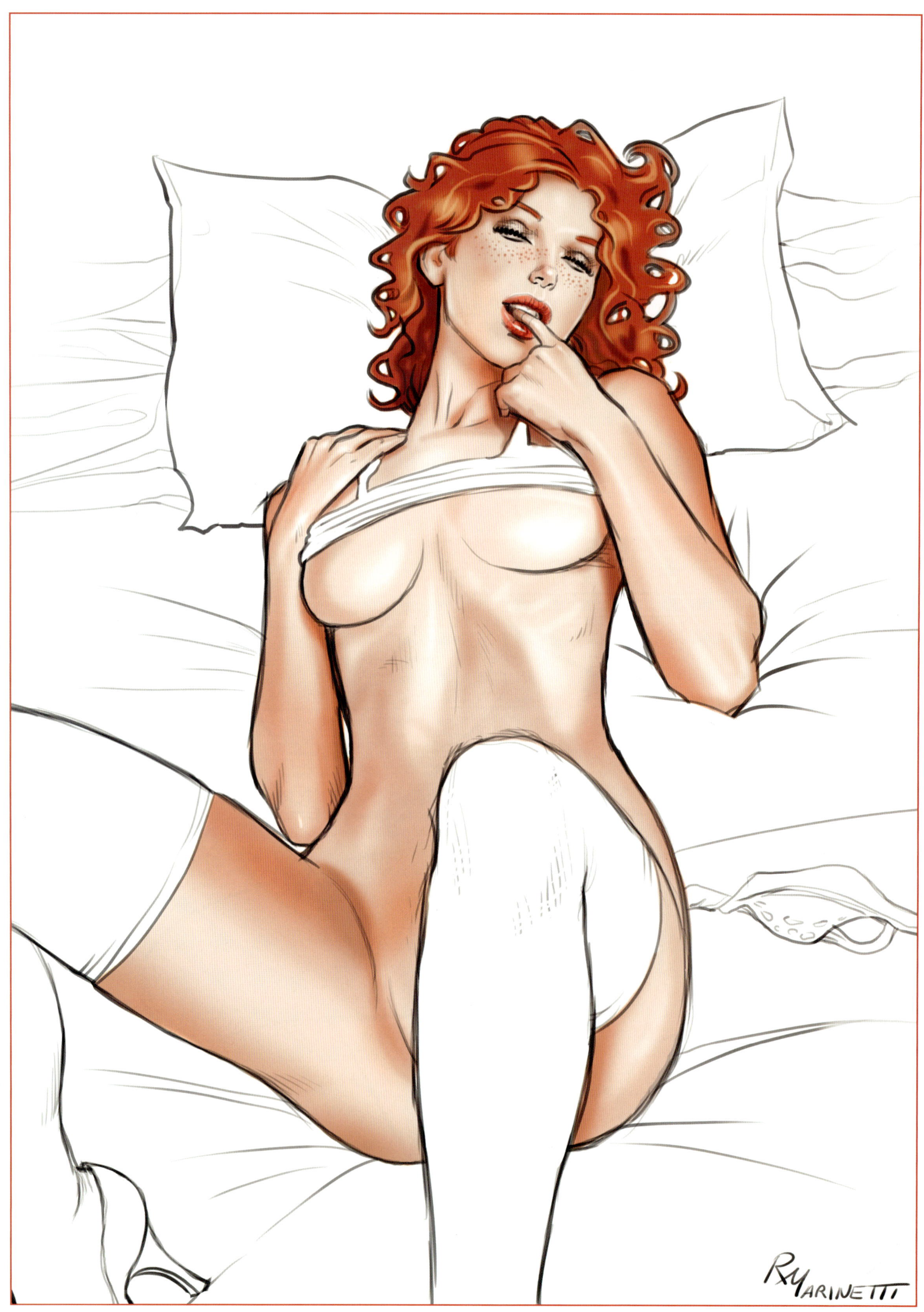

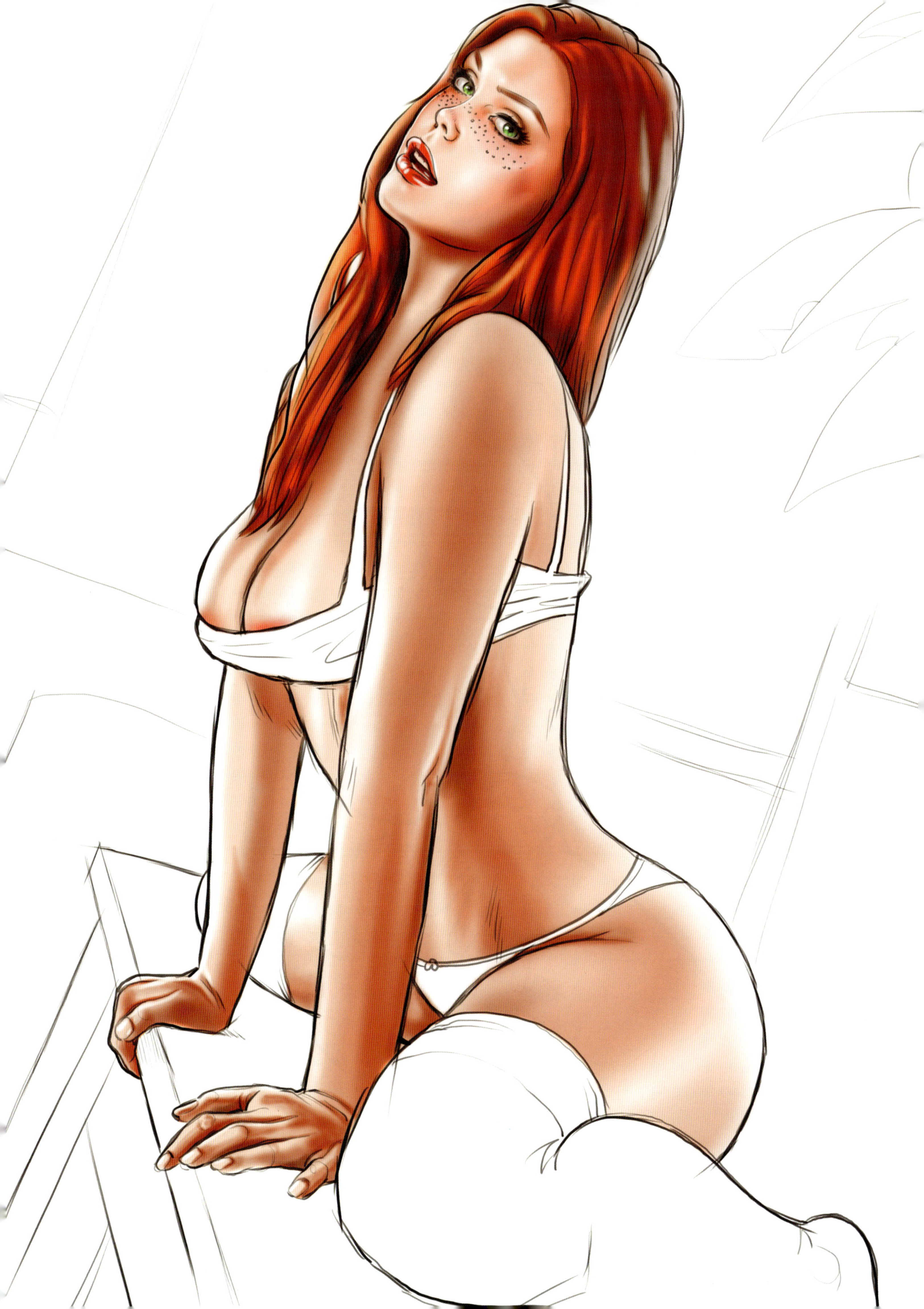

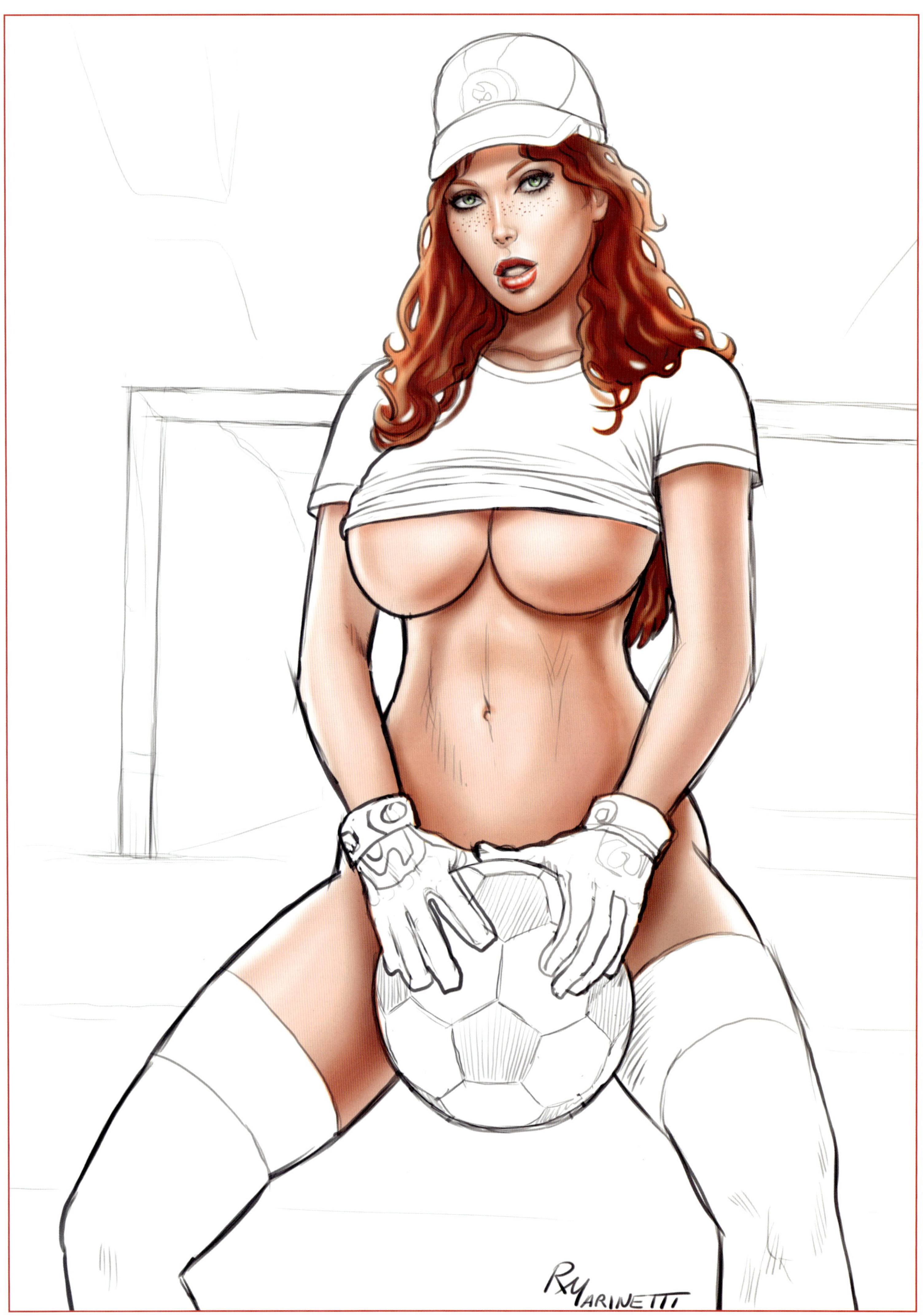
RXMARINETTI

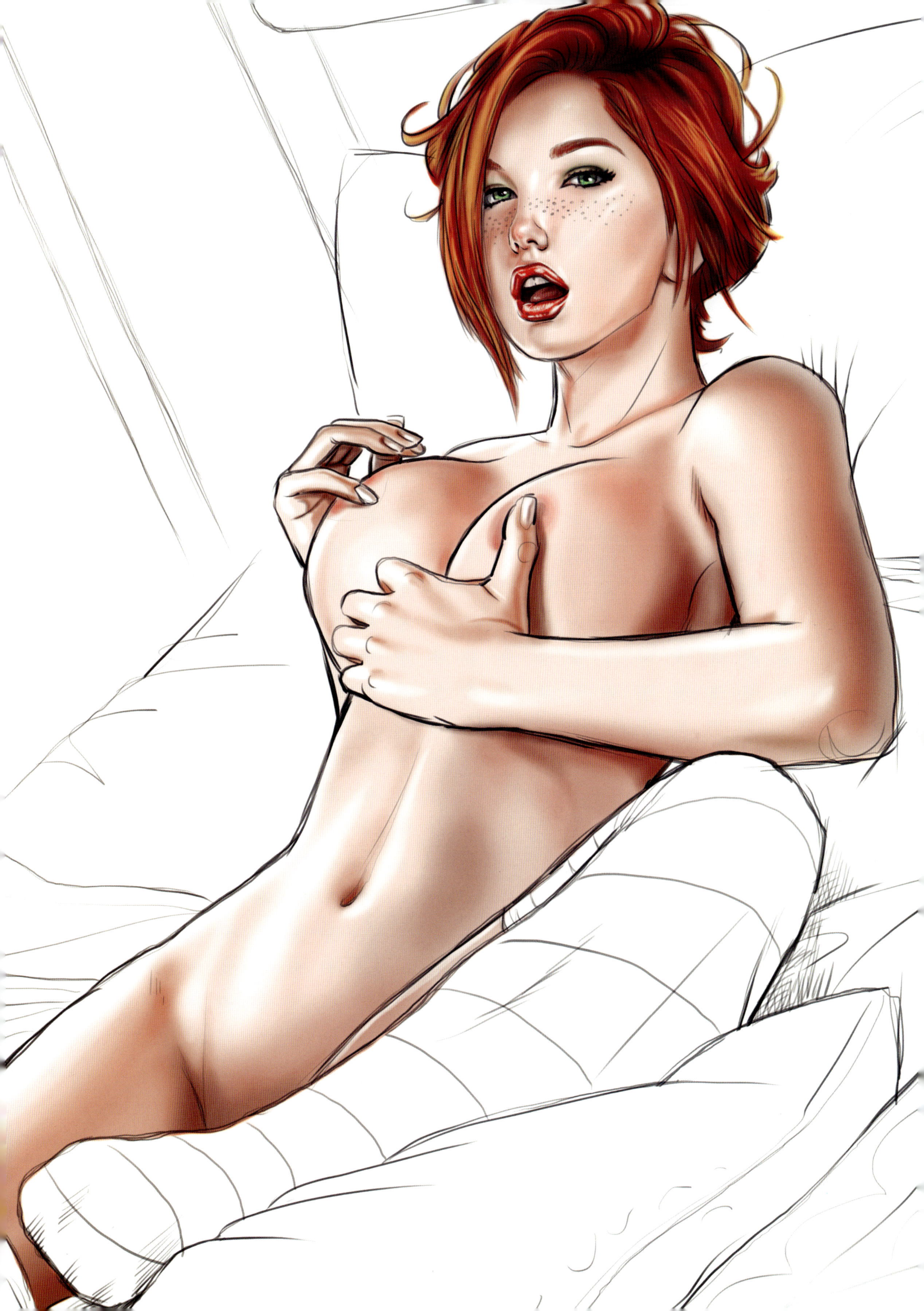

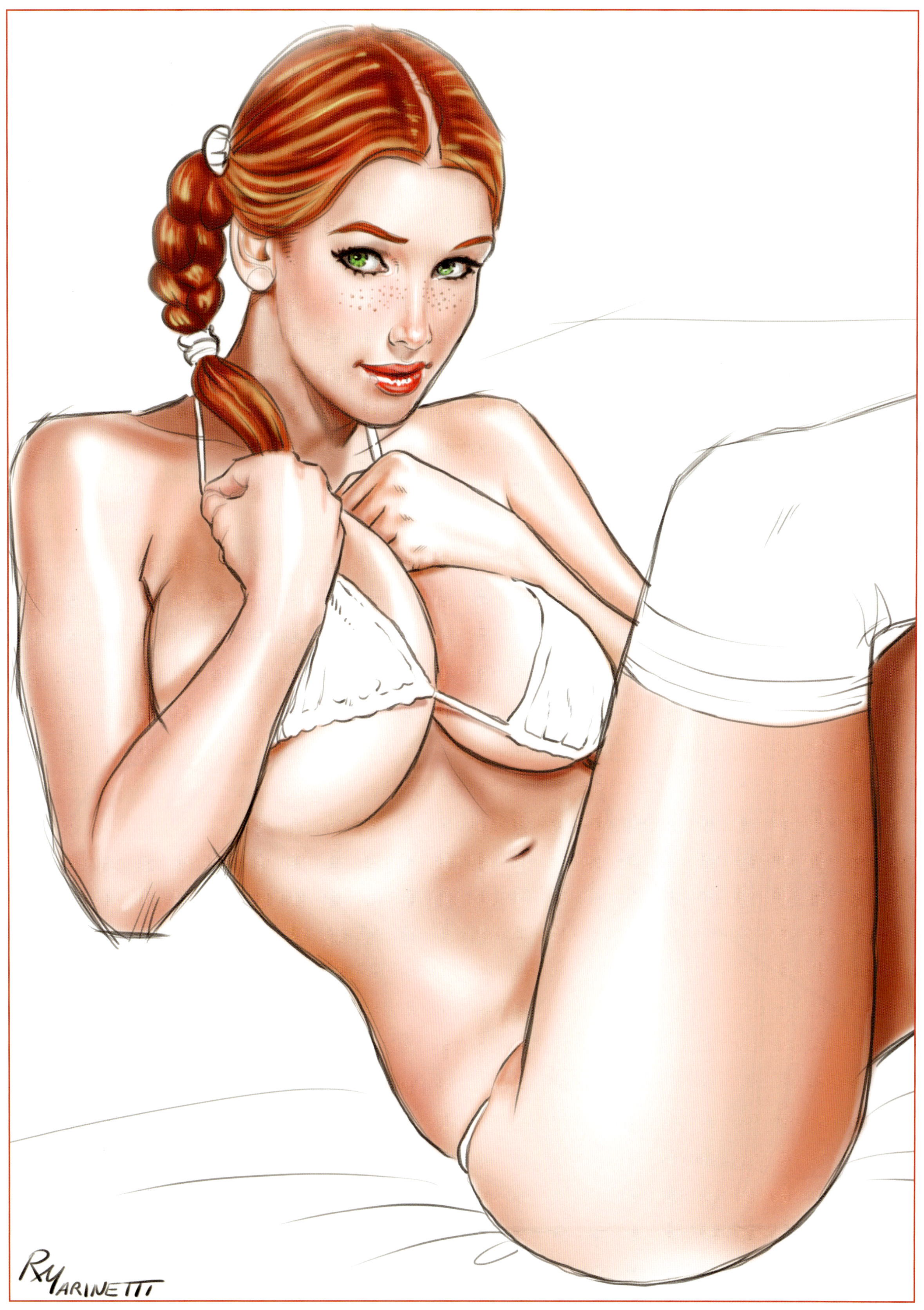

R.MARINETTI

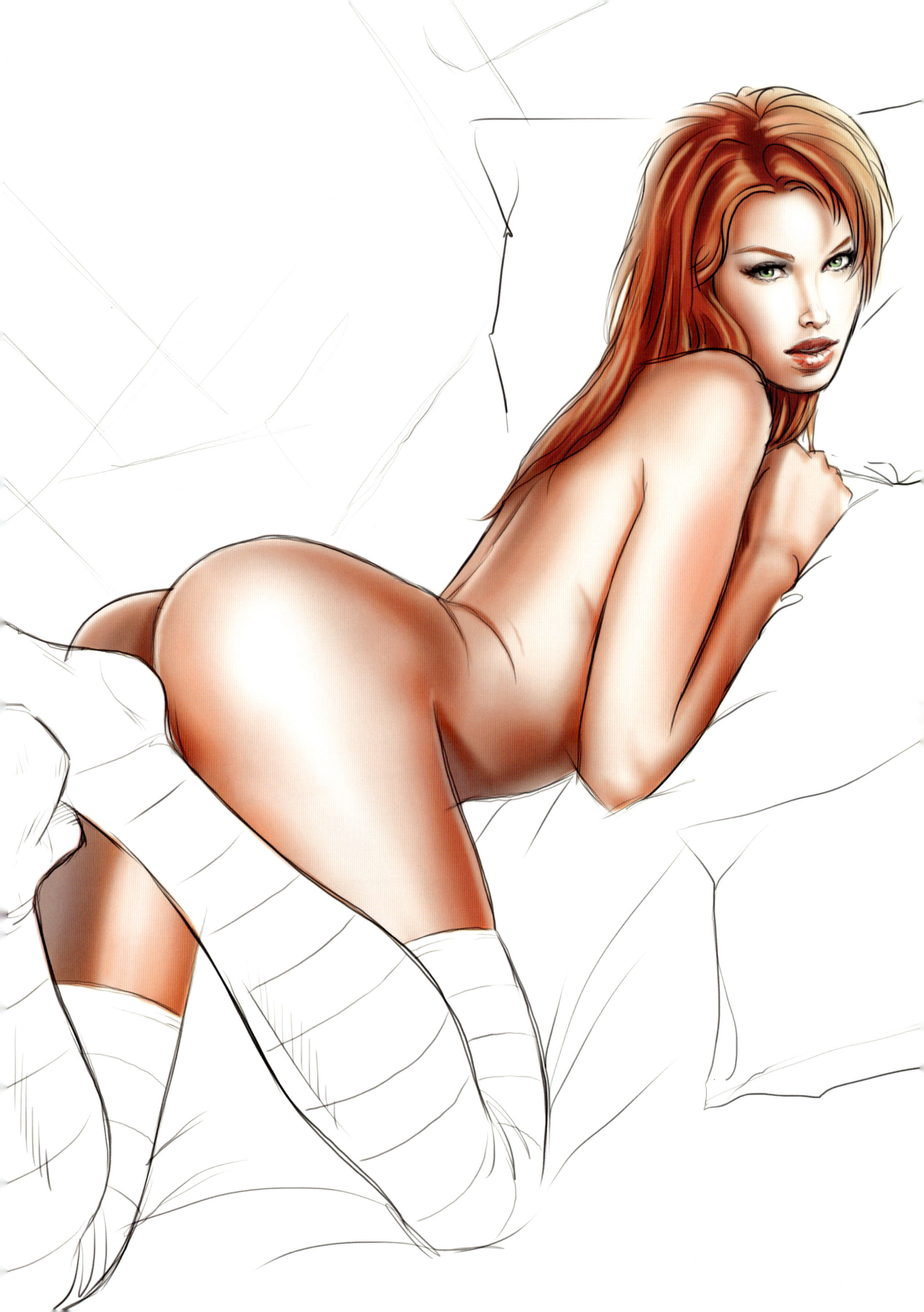

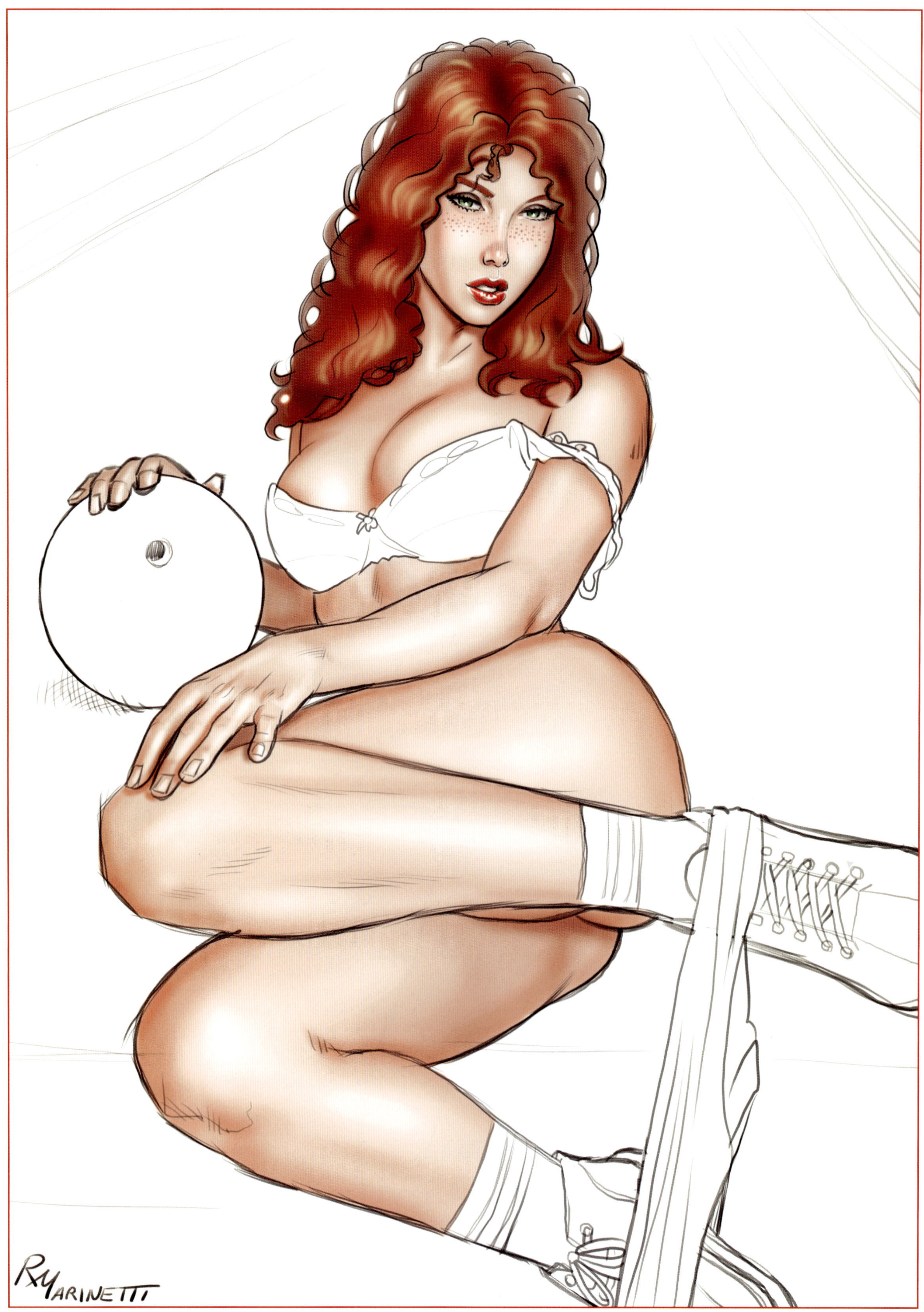

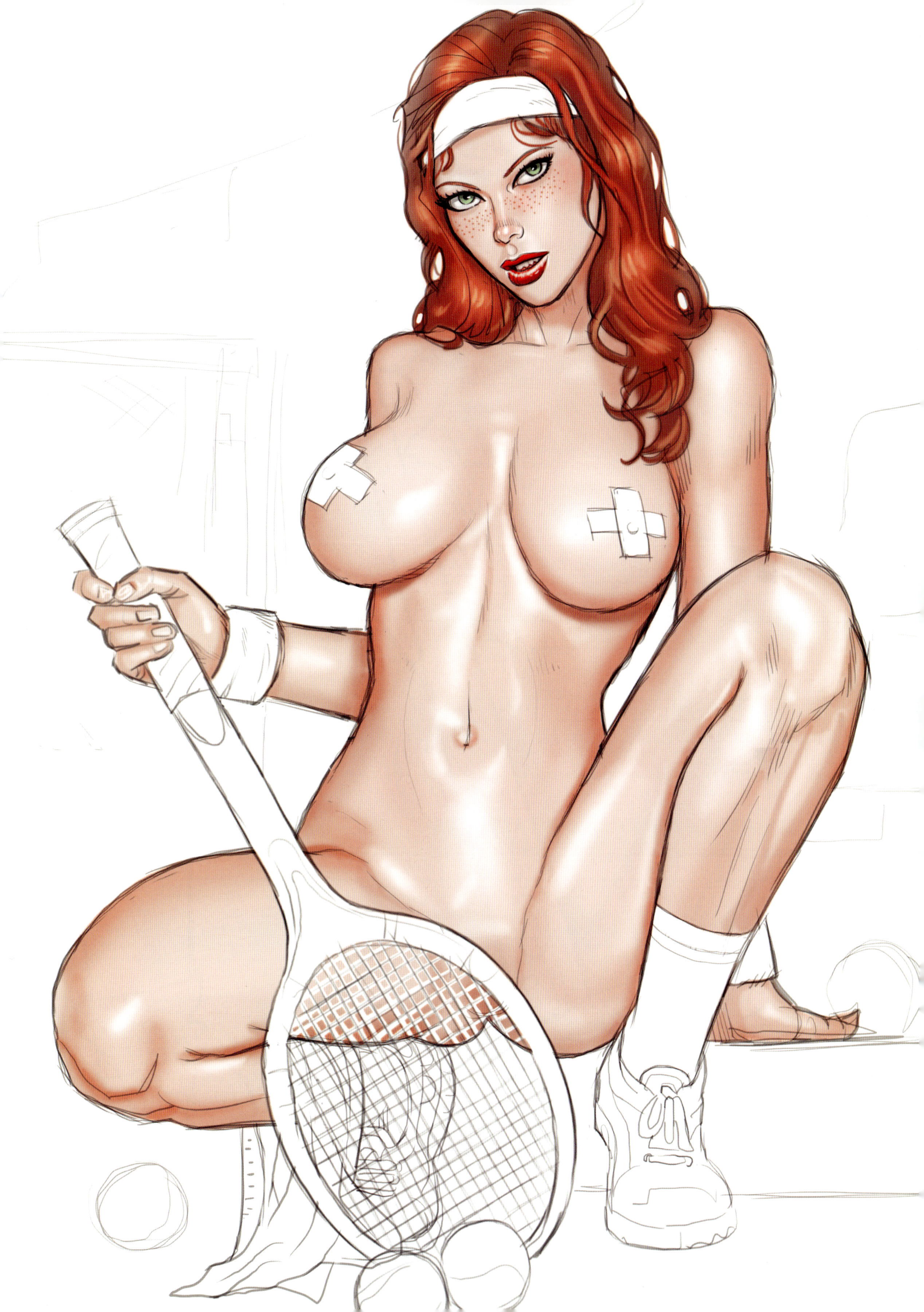

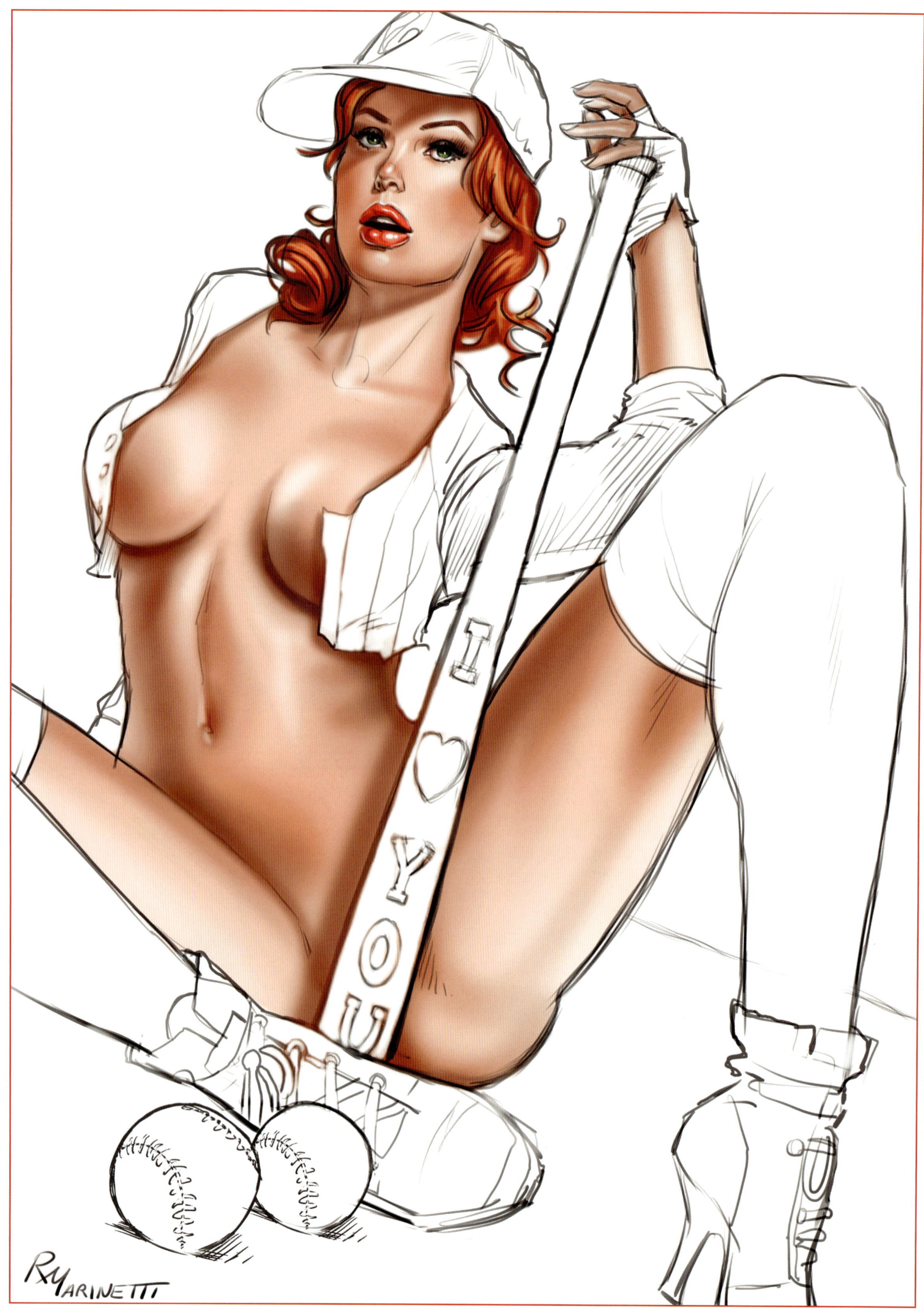
I
YOU

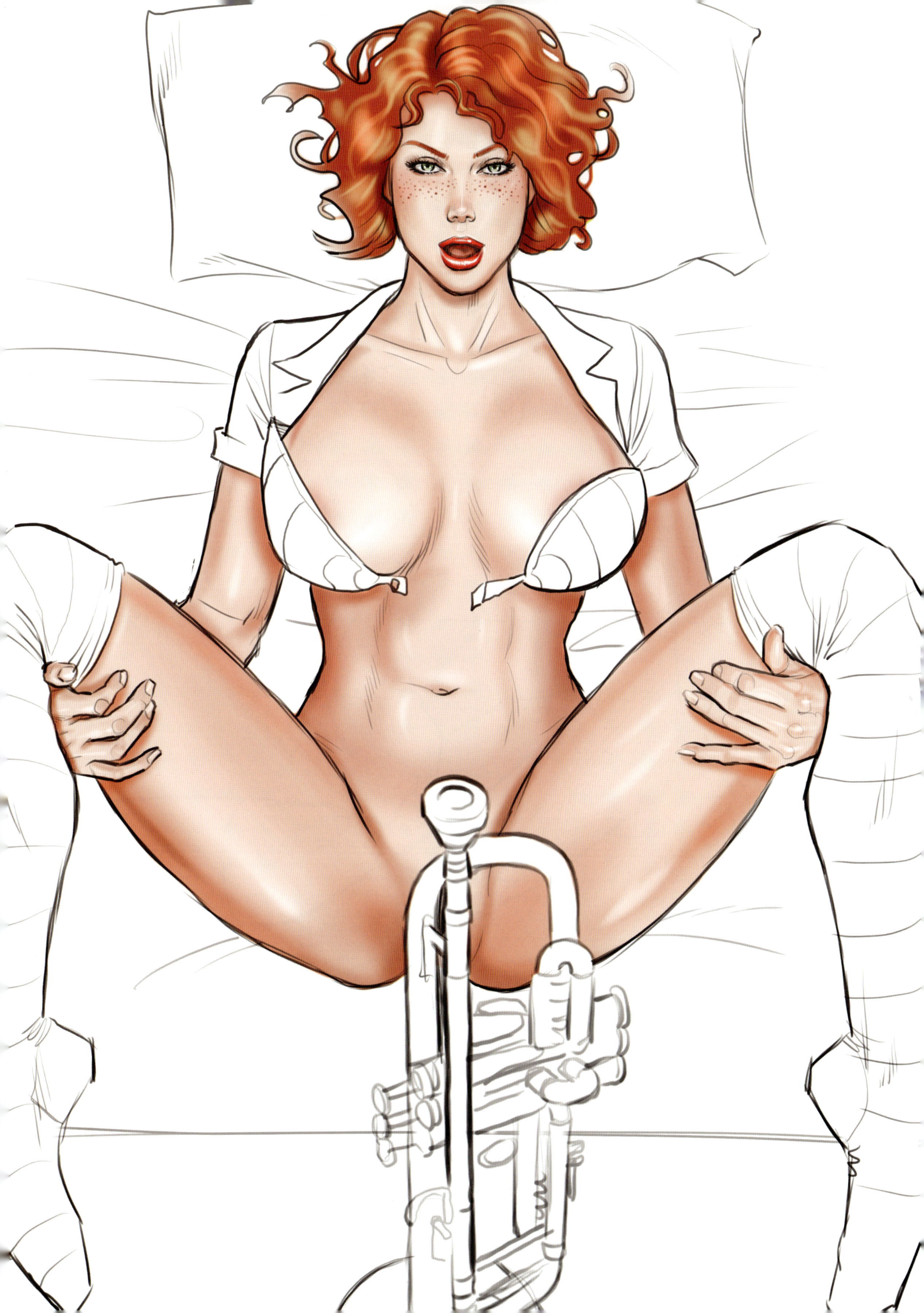

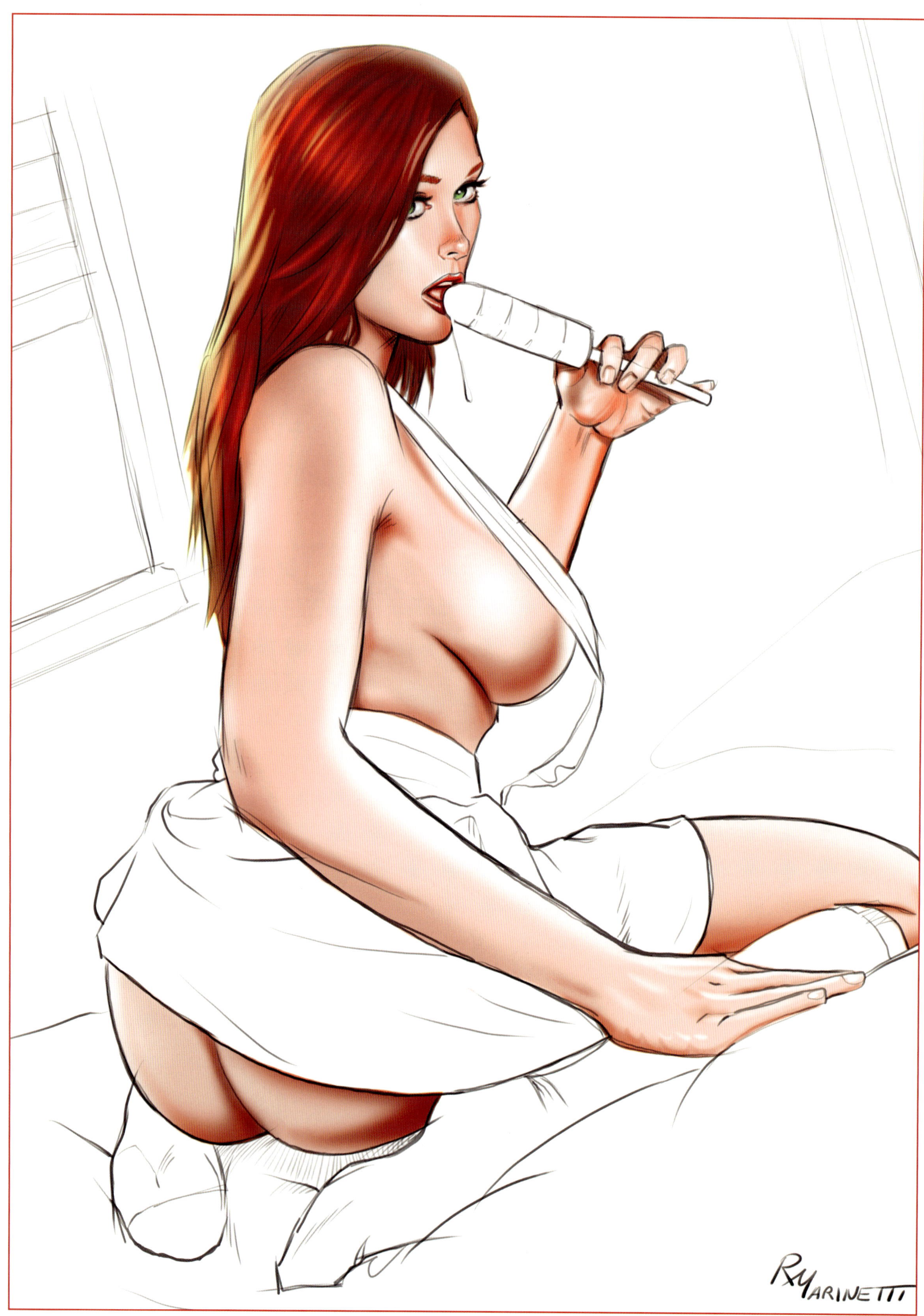
RMARINETTI

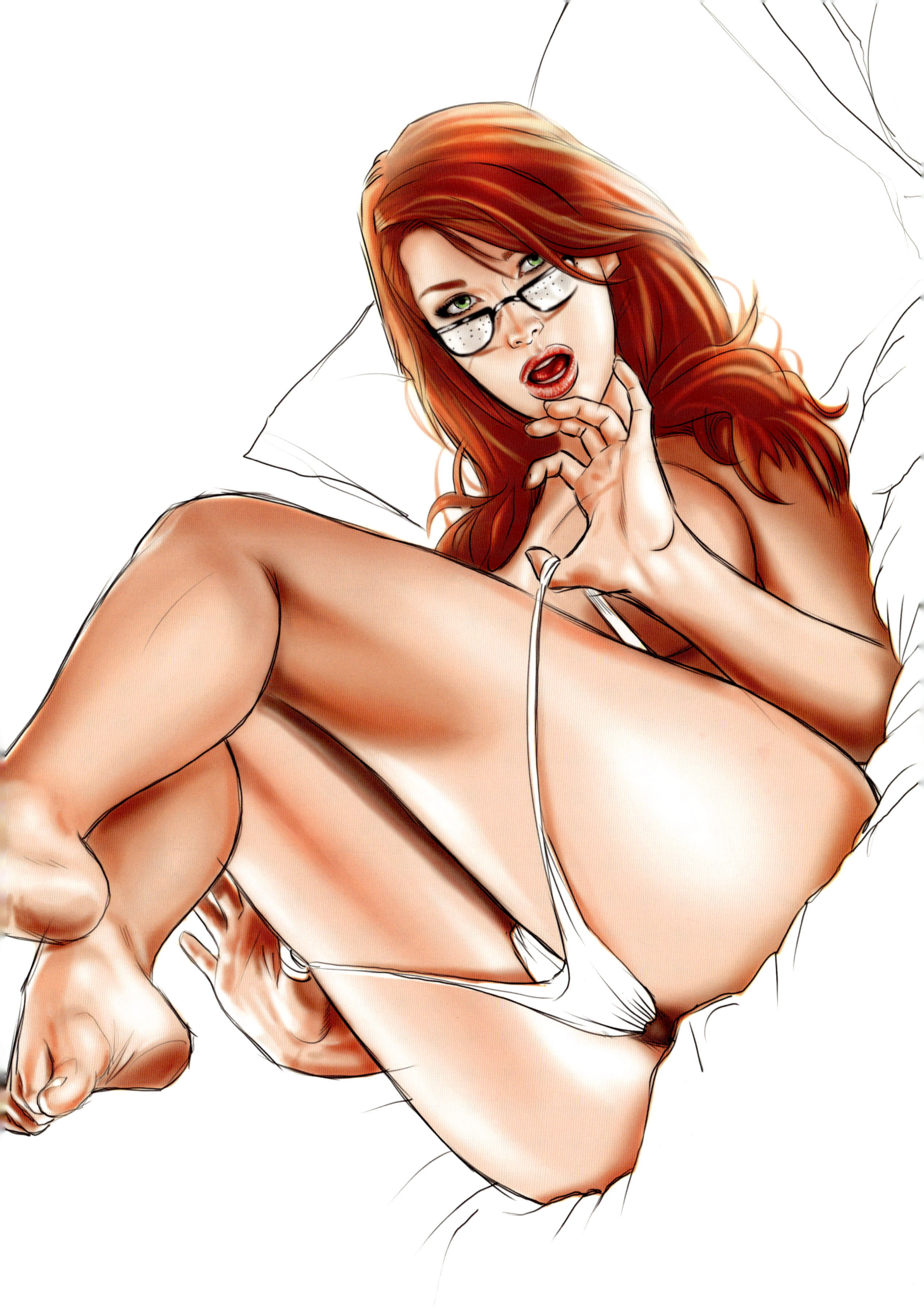

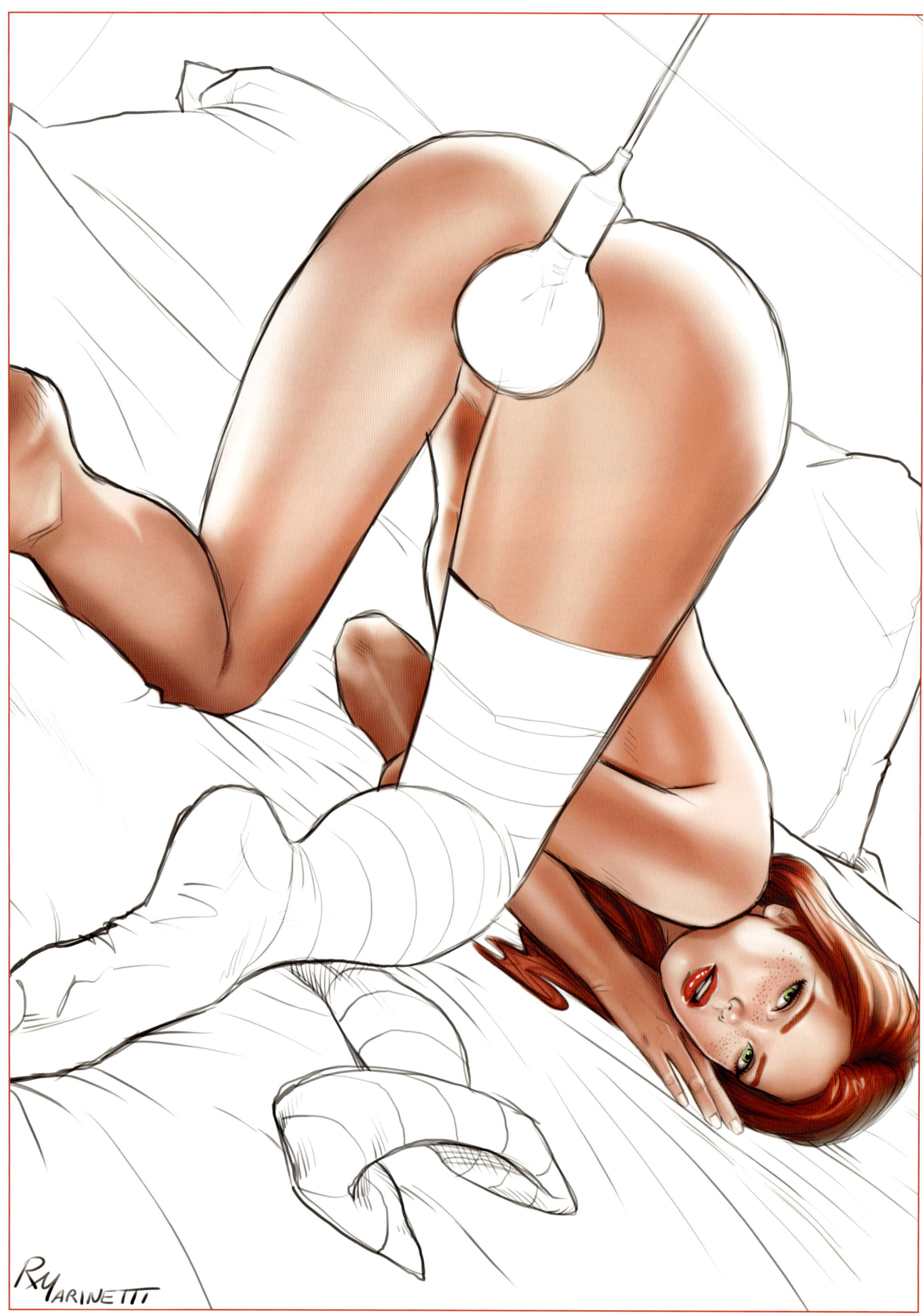
RMARINETTI

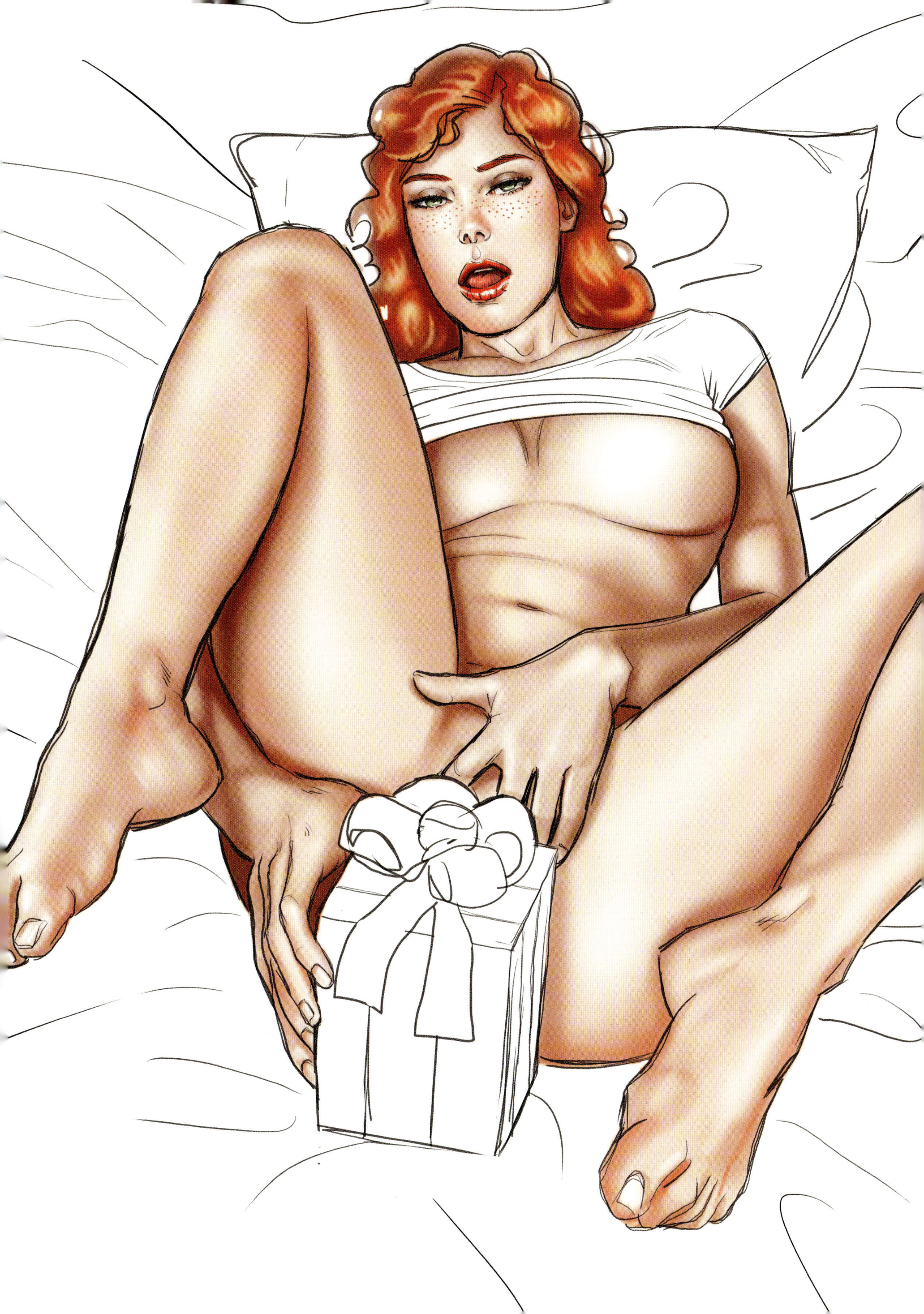

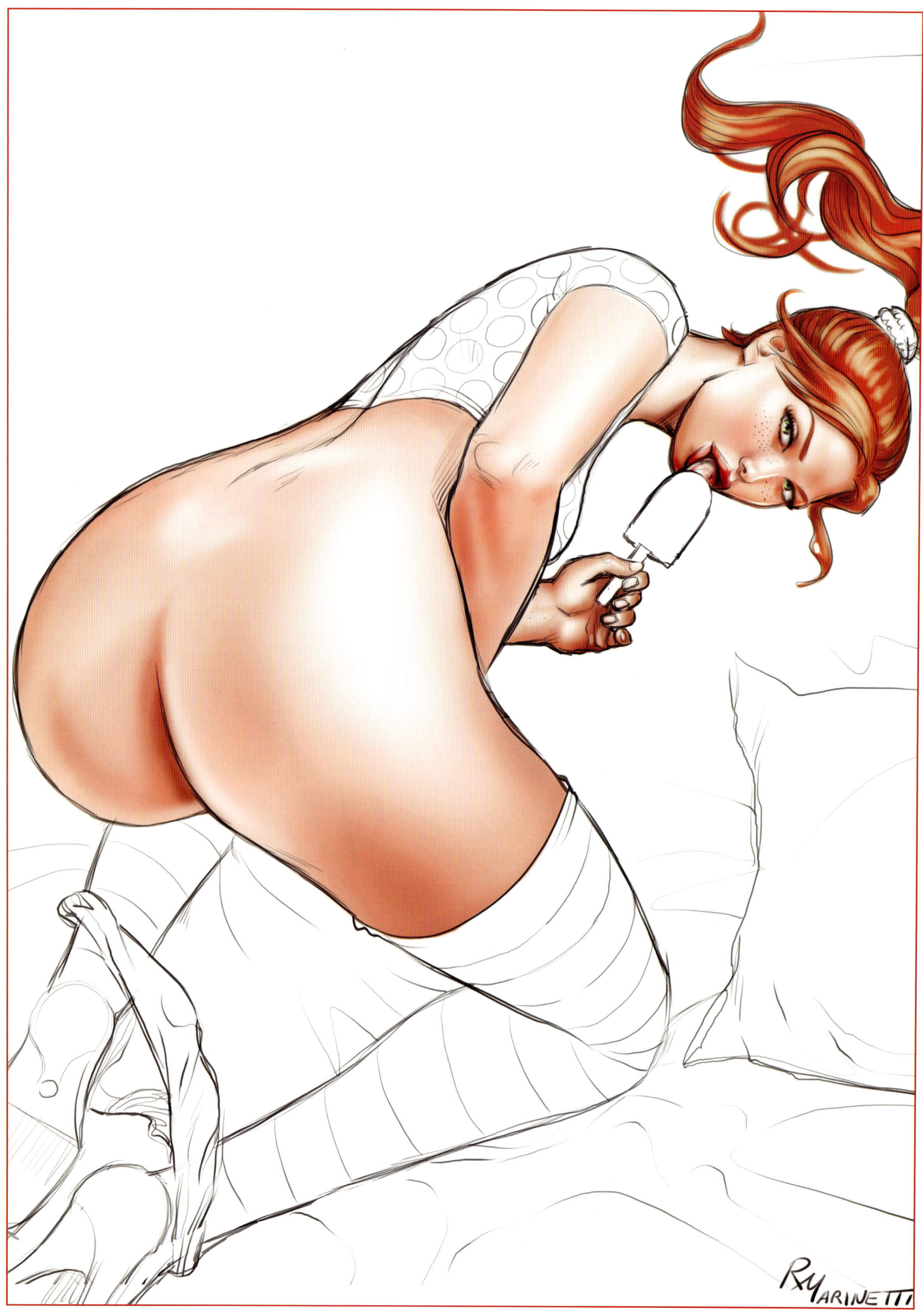
RMARINETTI

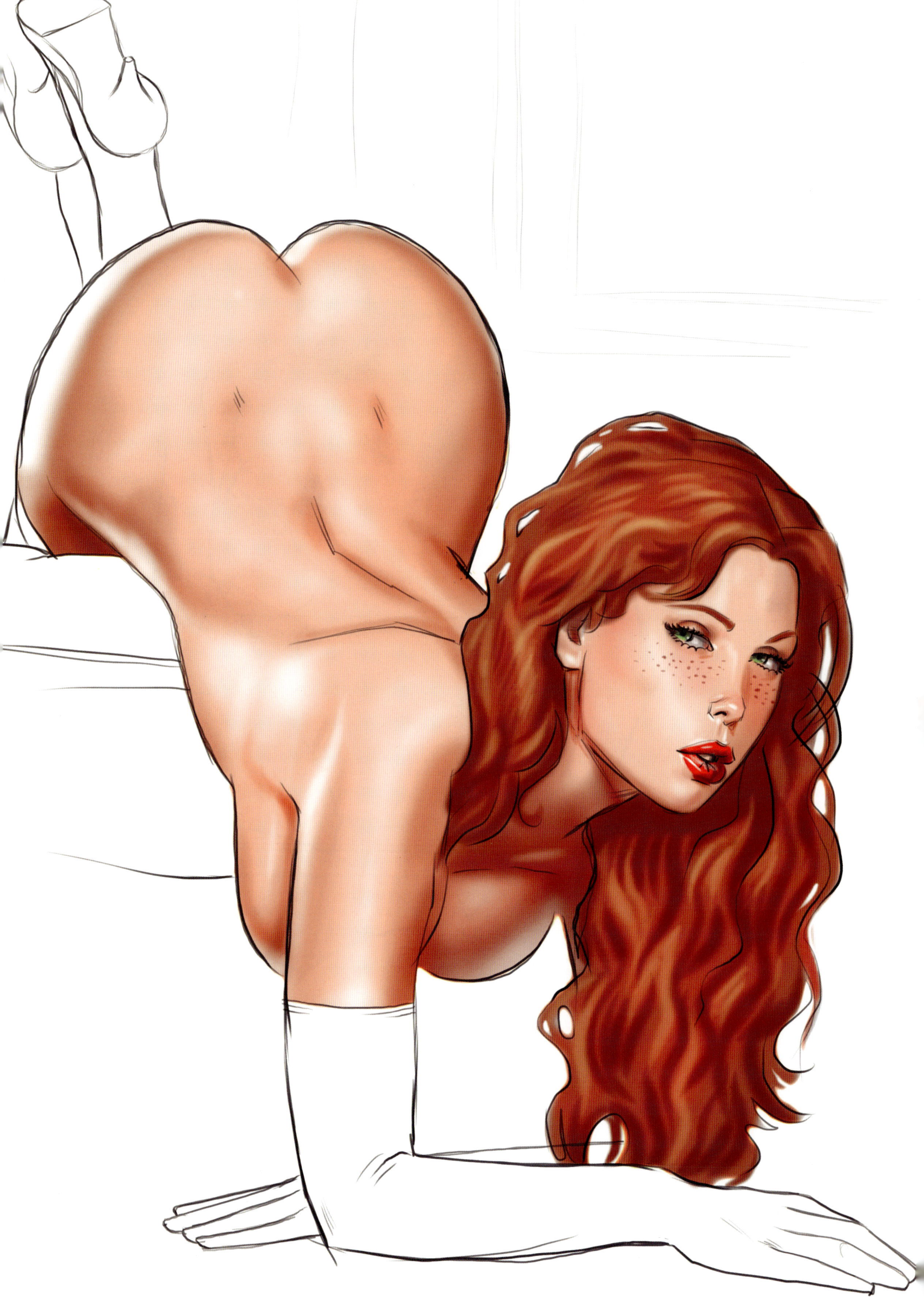

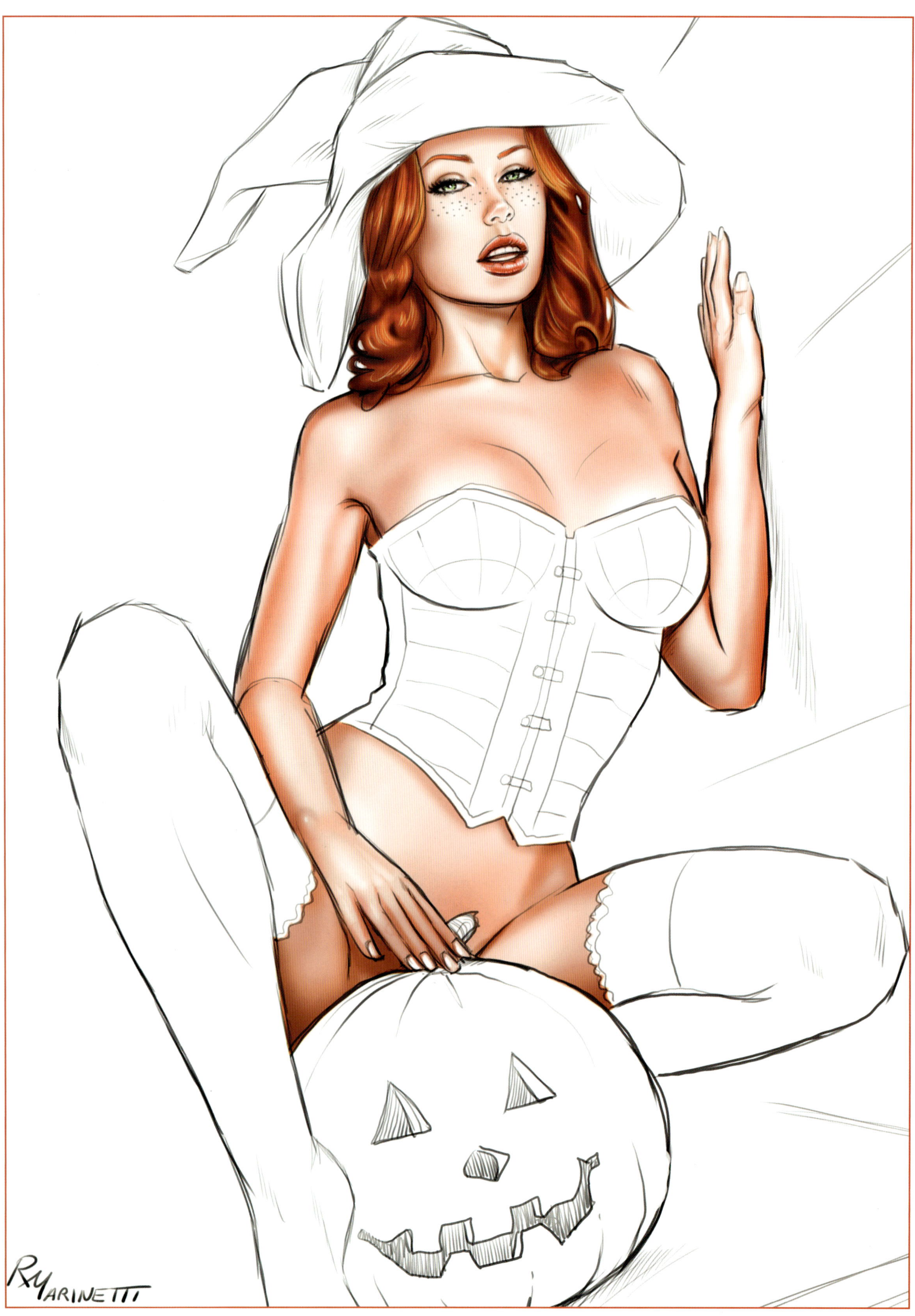

RMARINETTI

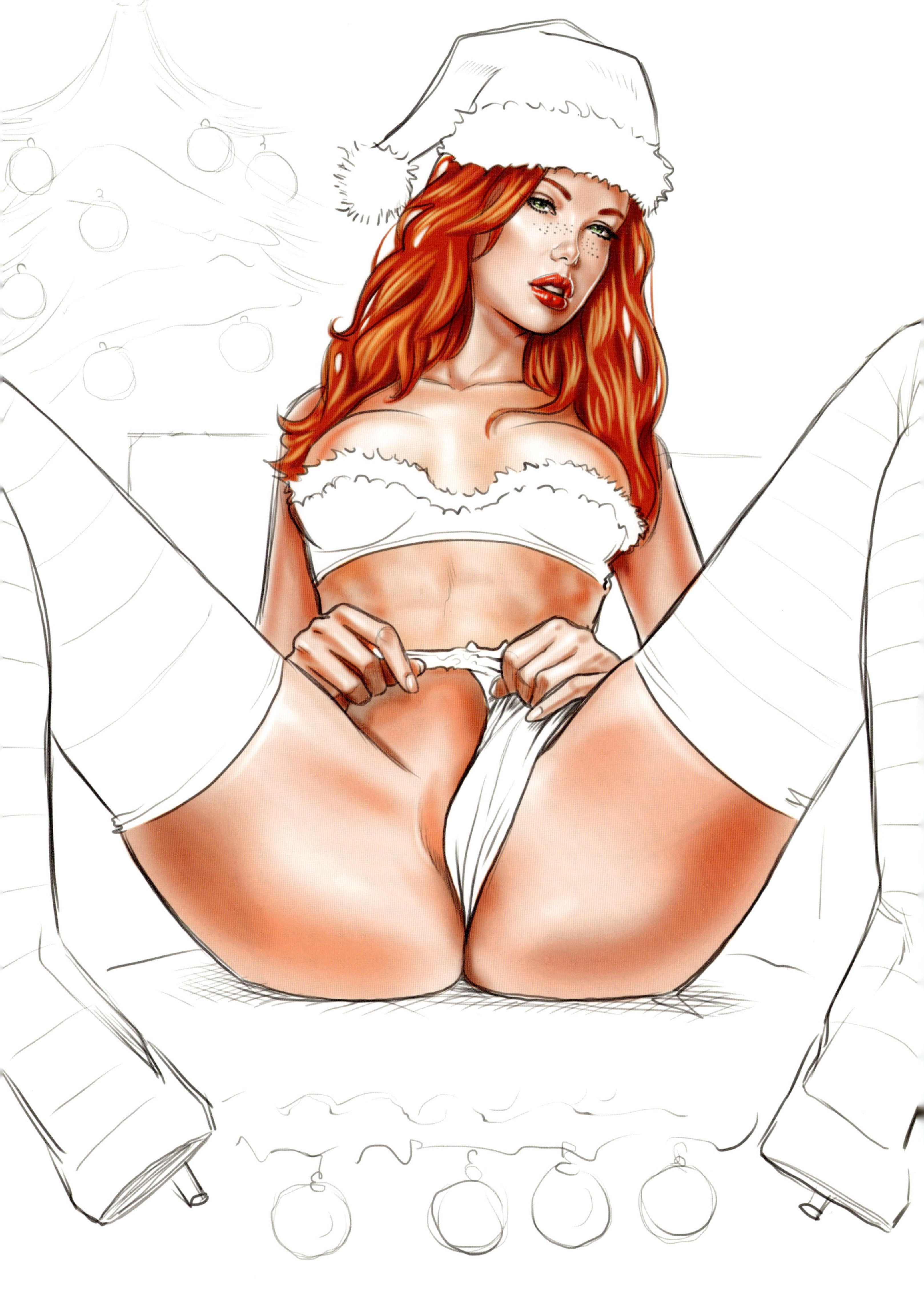

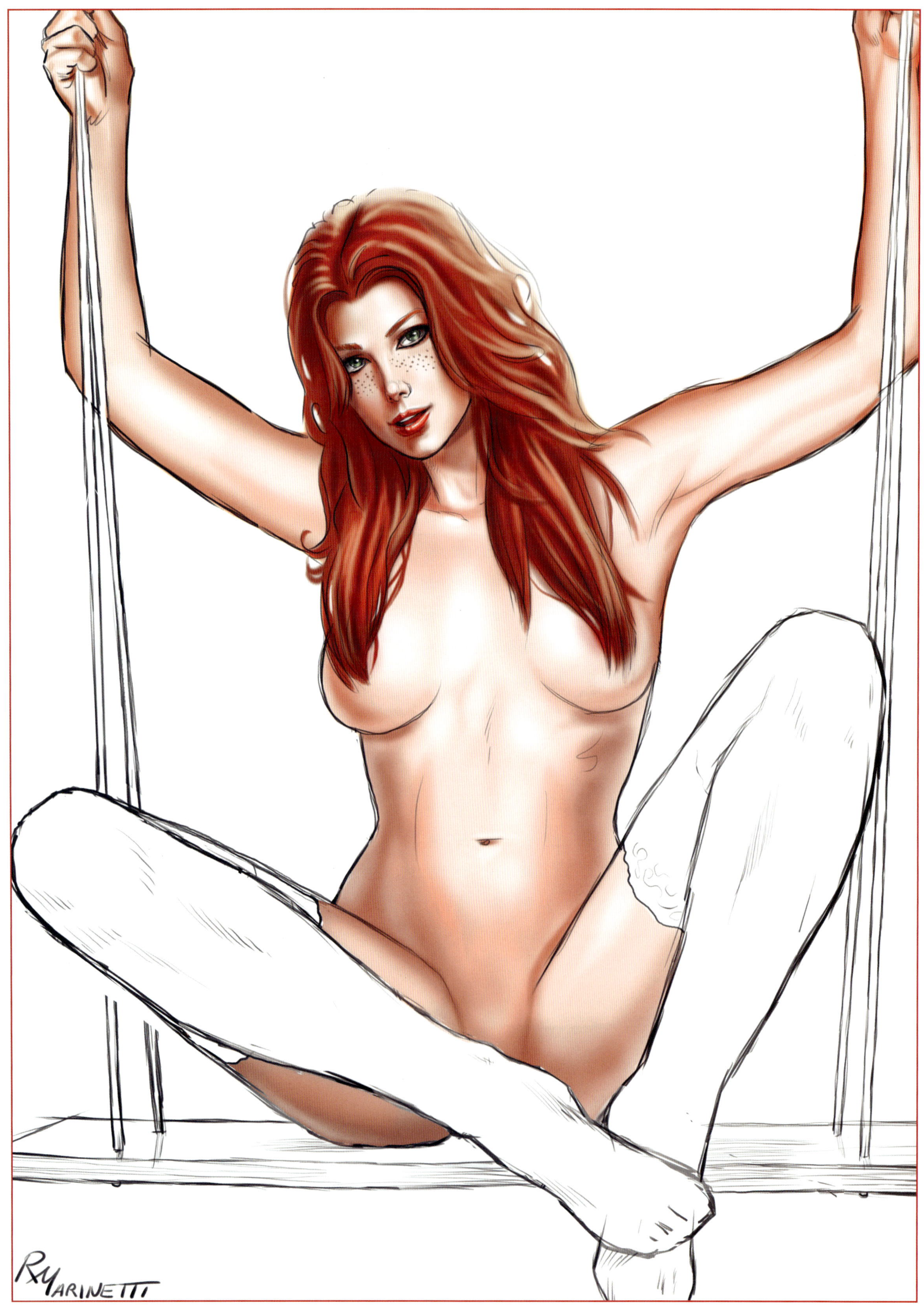
RM MARINETTI

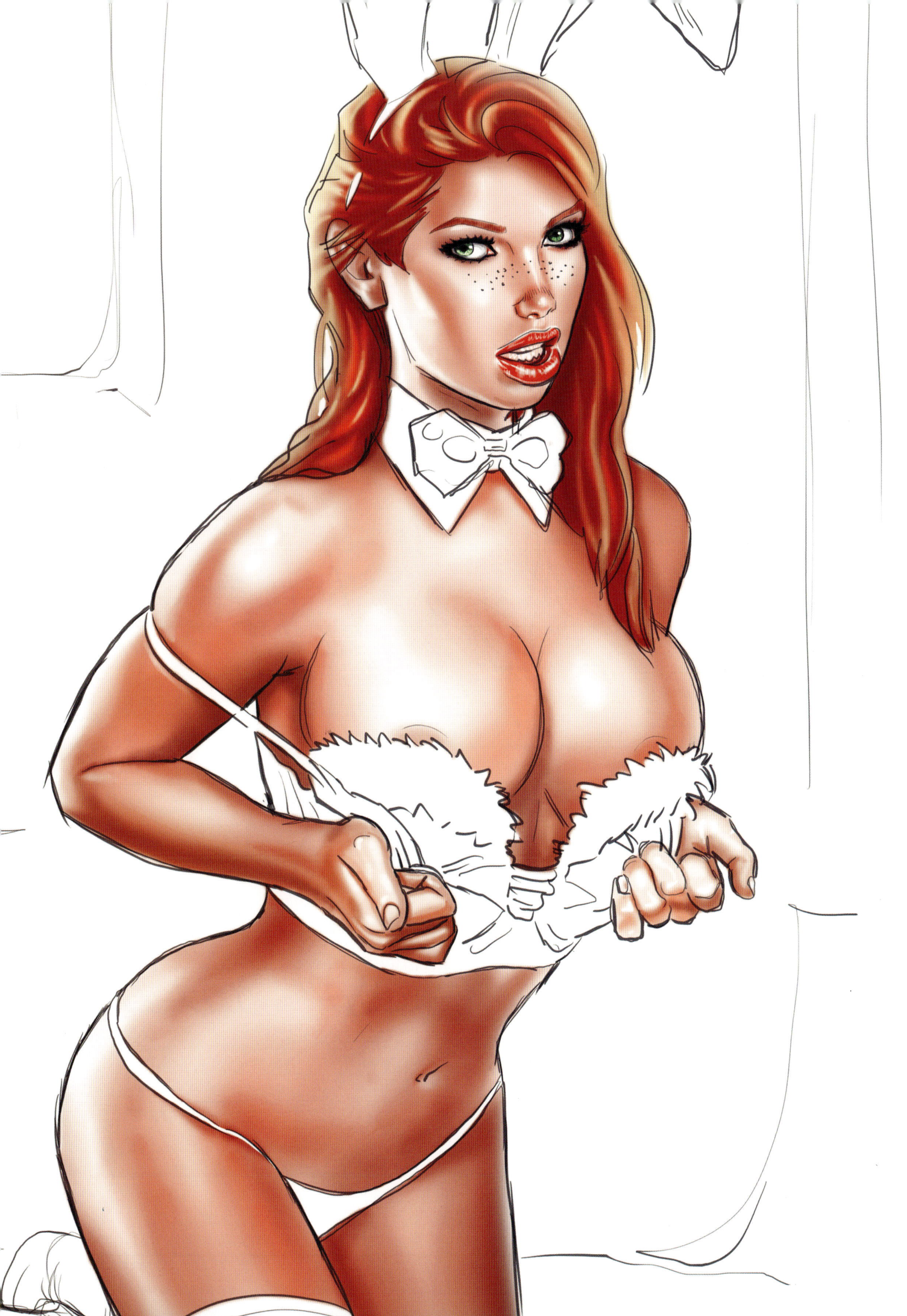

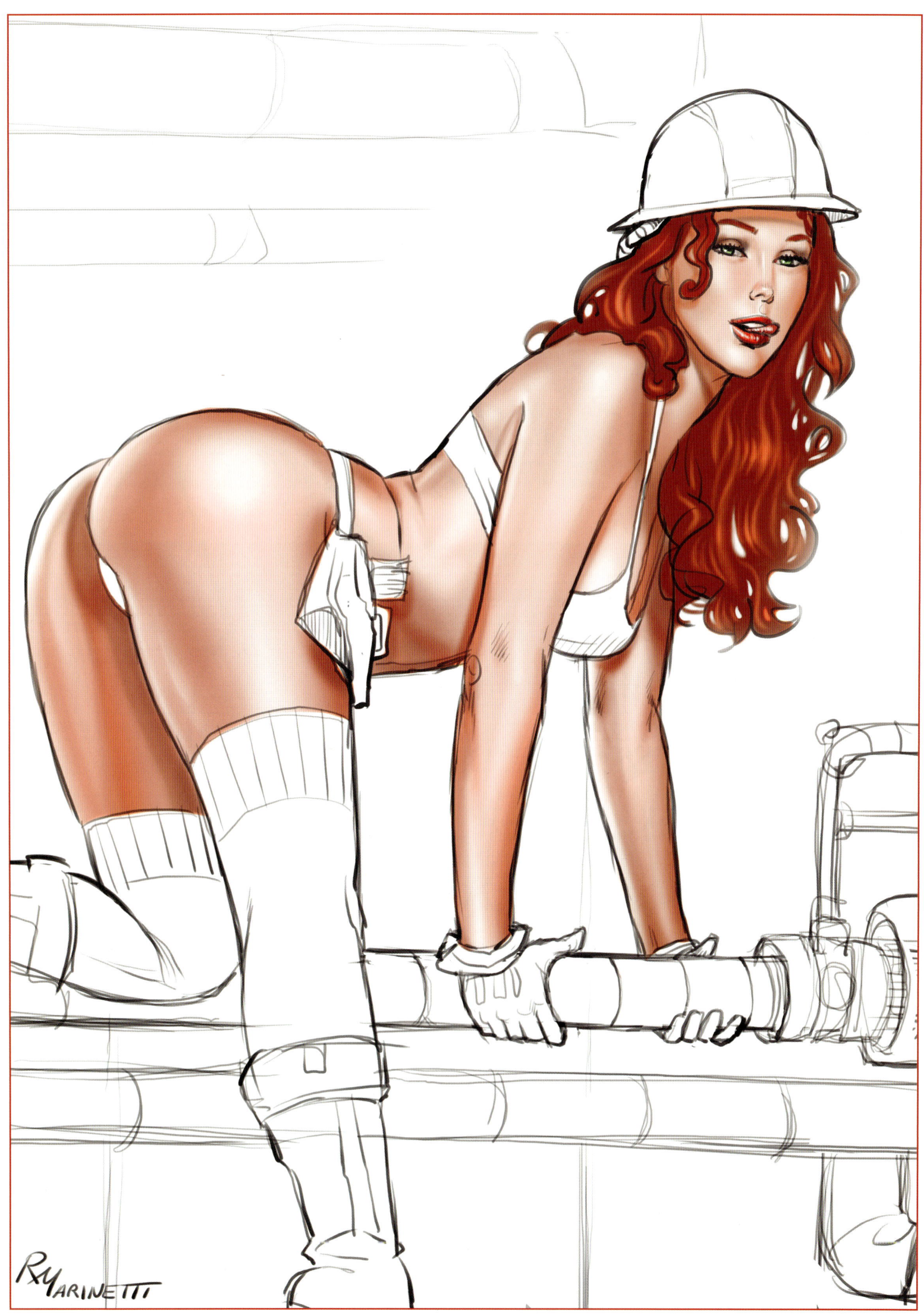
RxMARINETTI

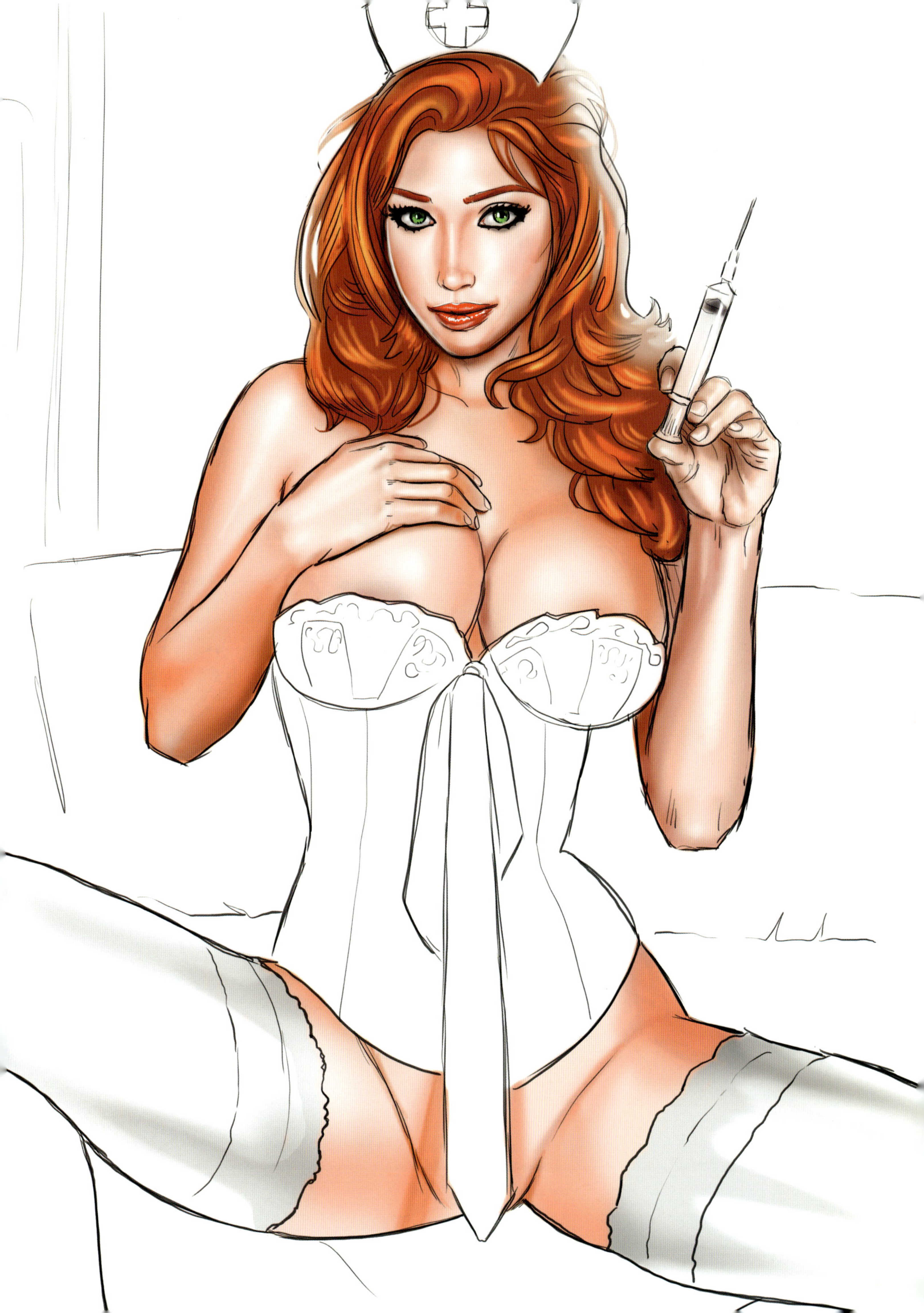

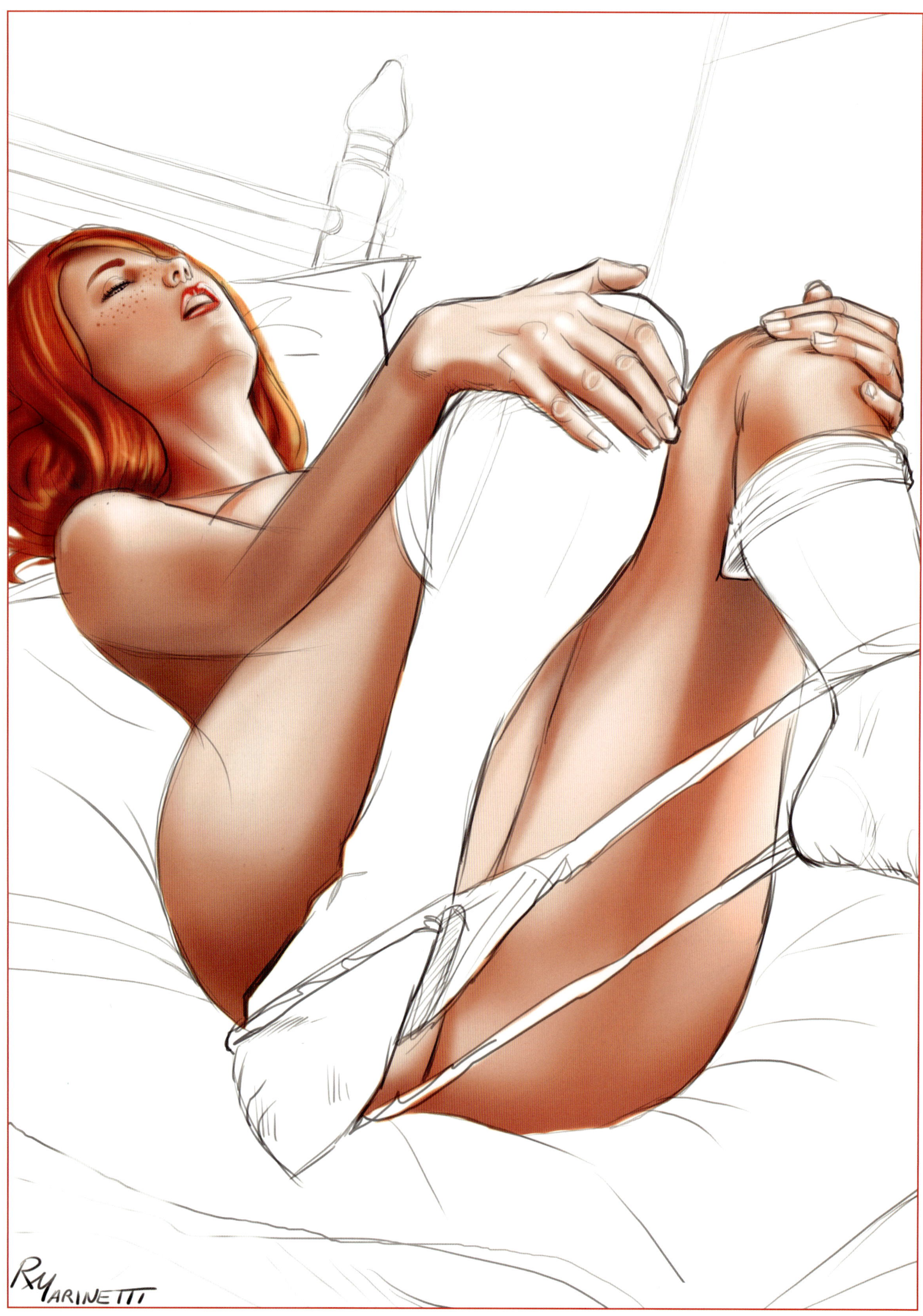
RMarinetti

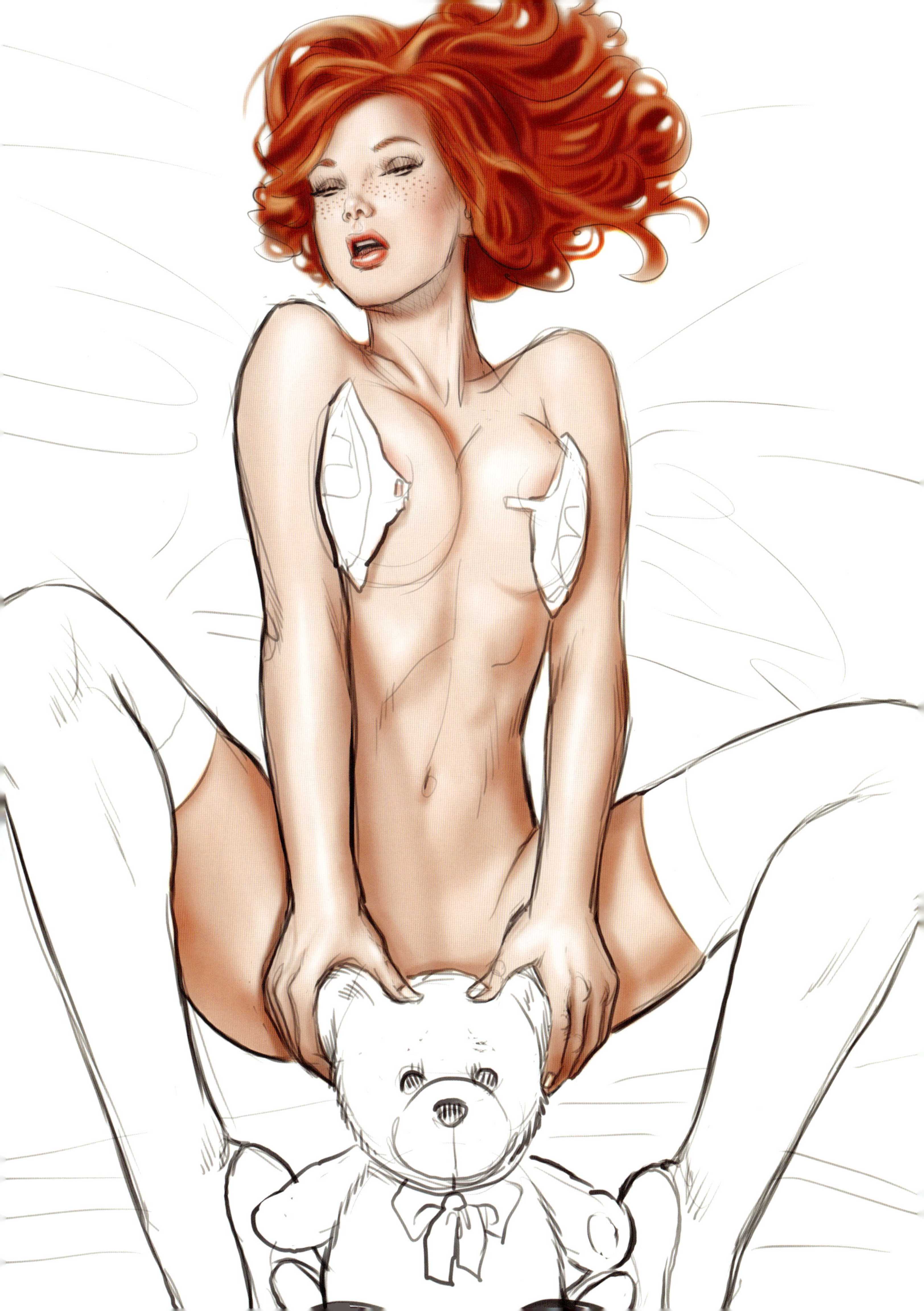

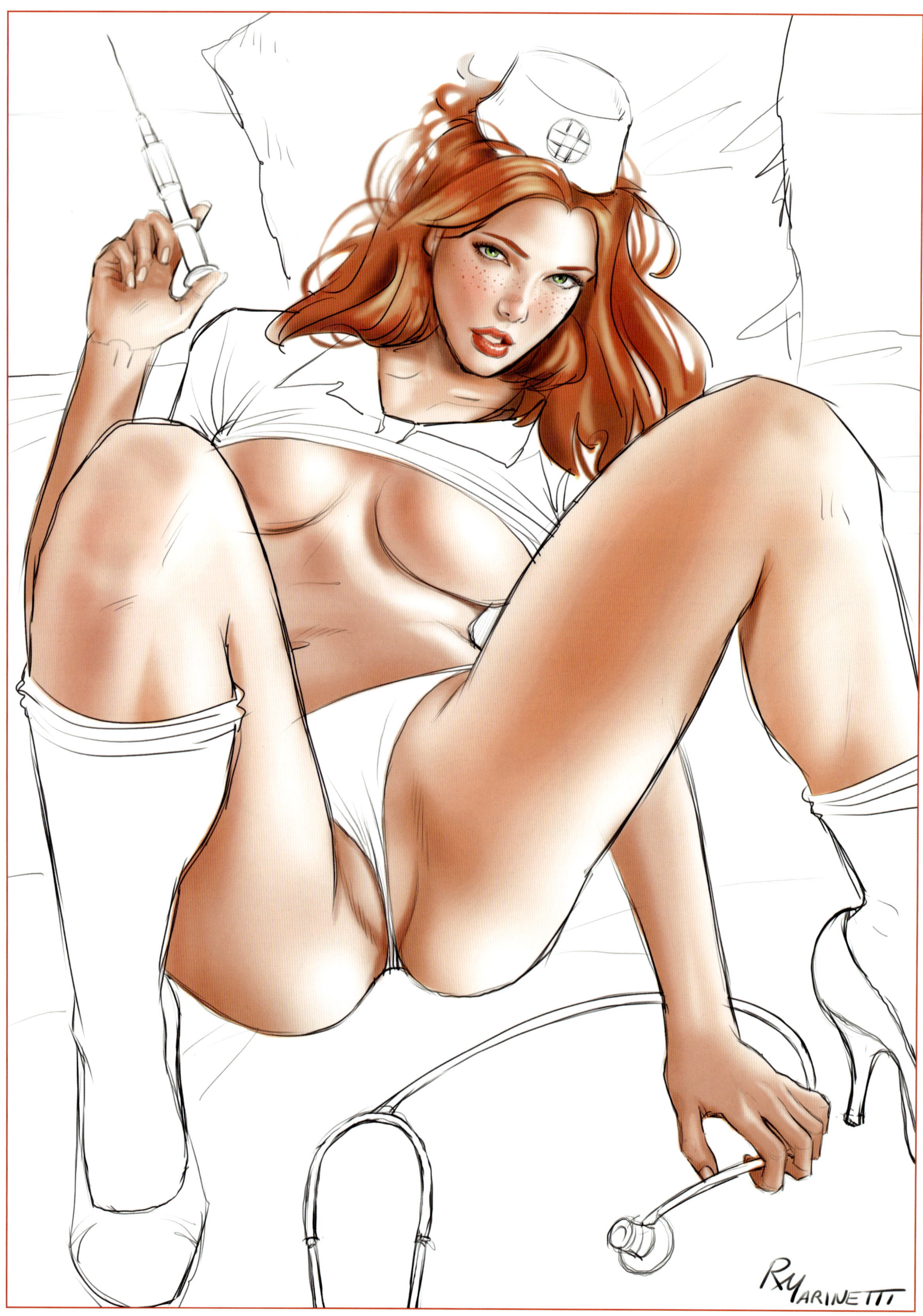
RMARINETTI

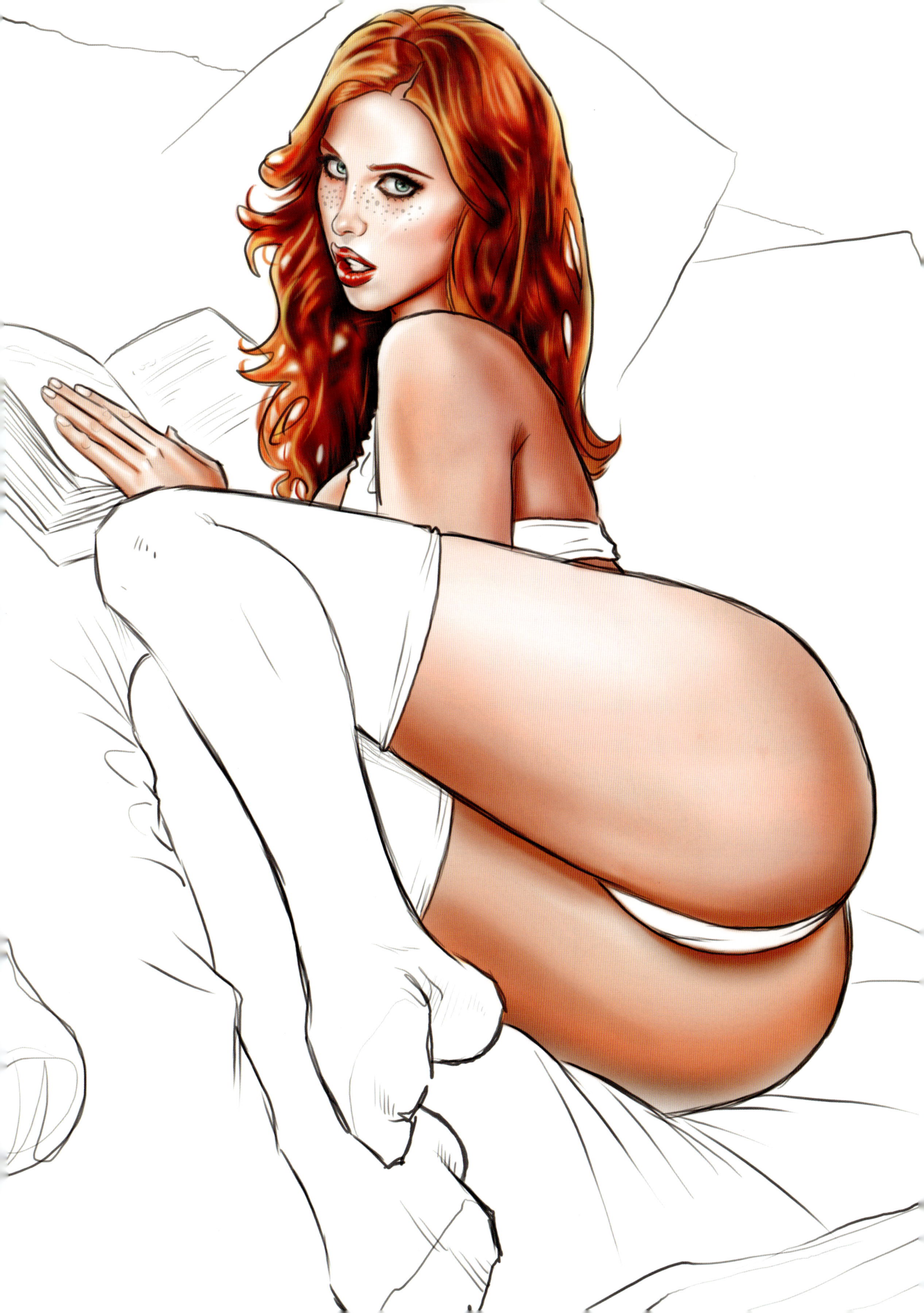

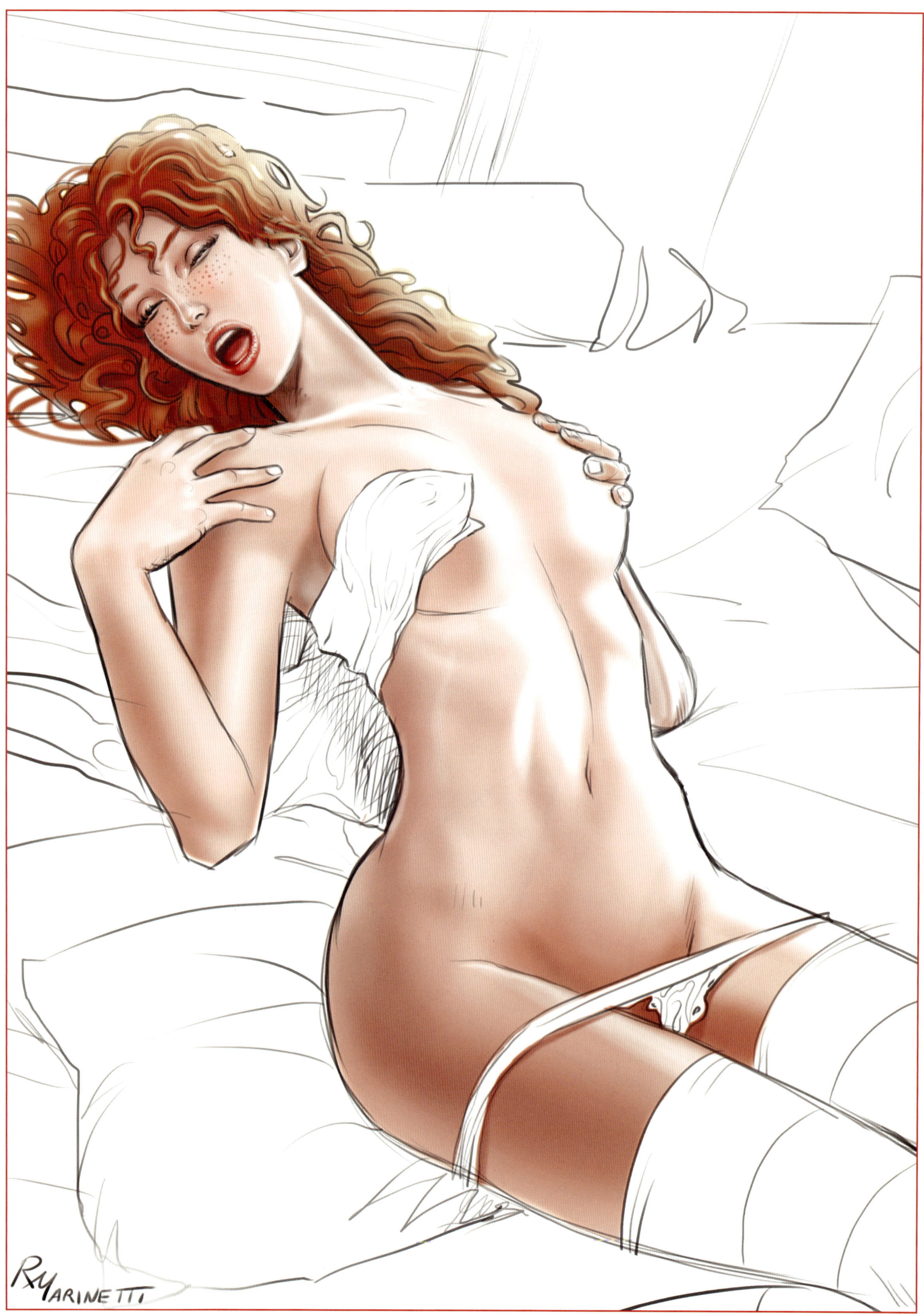

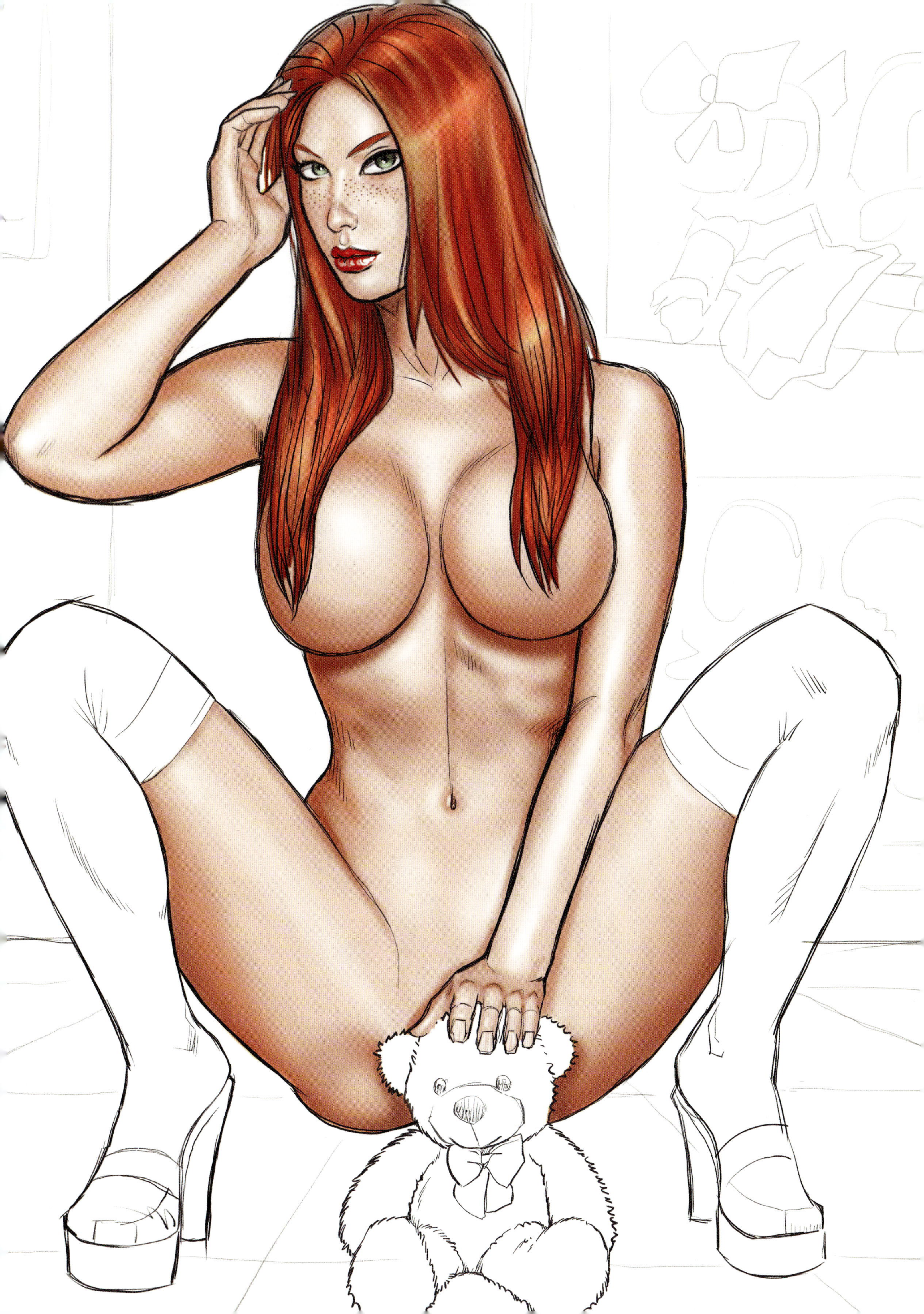

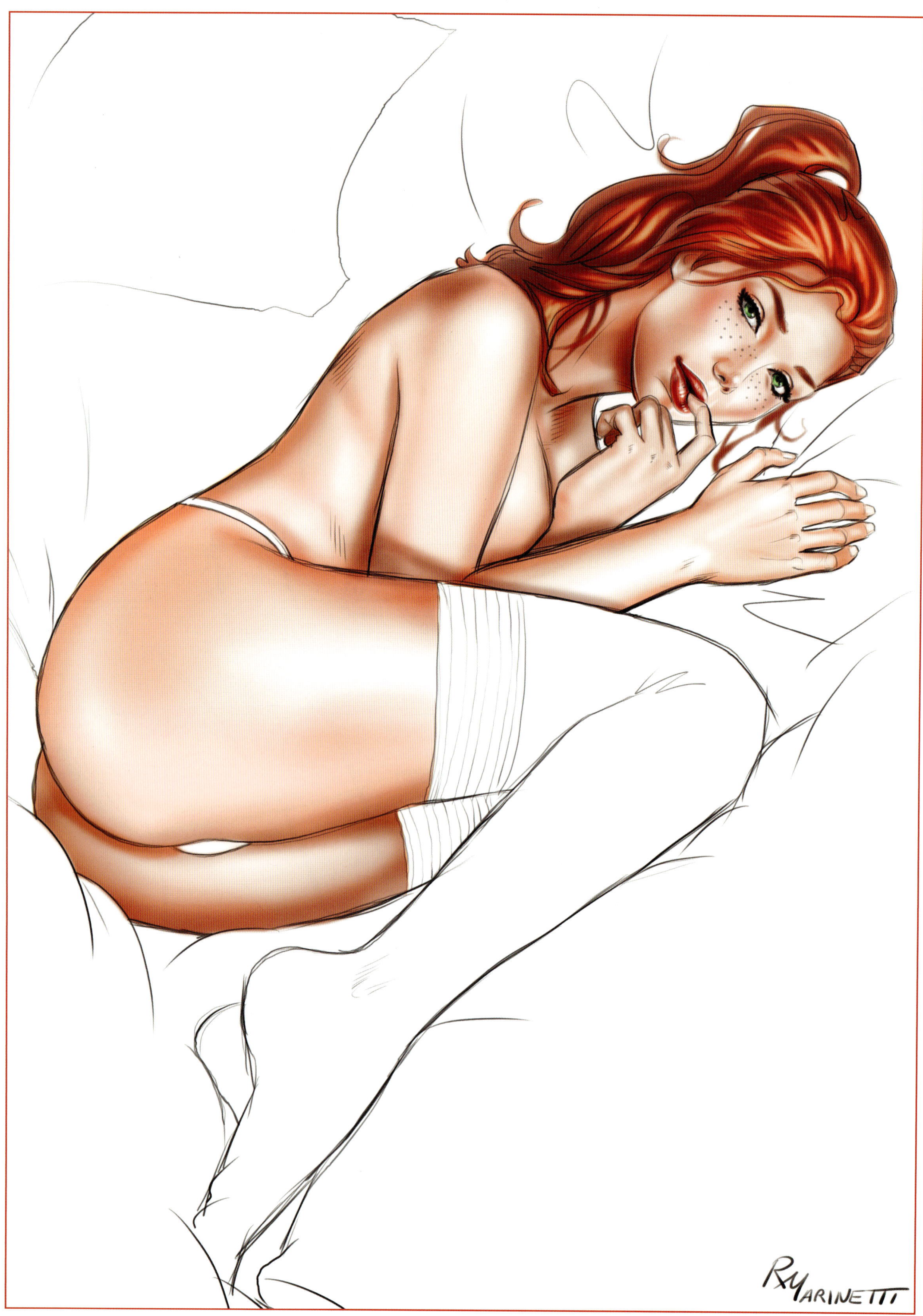

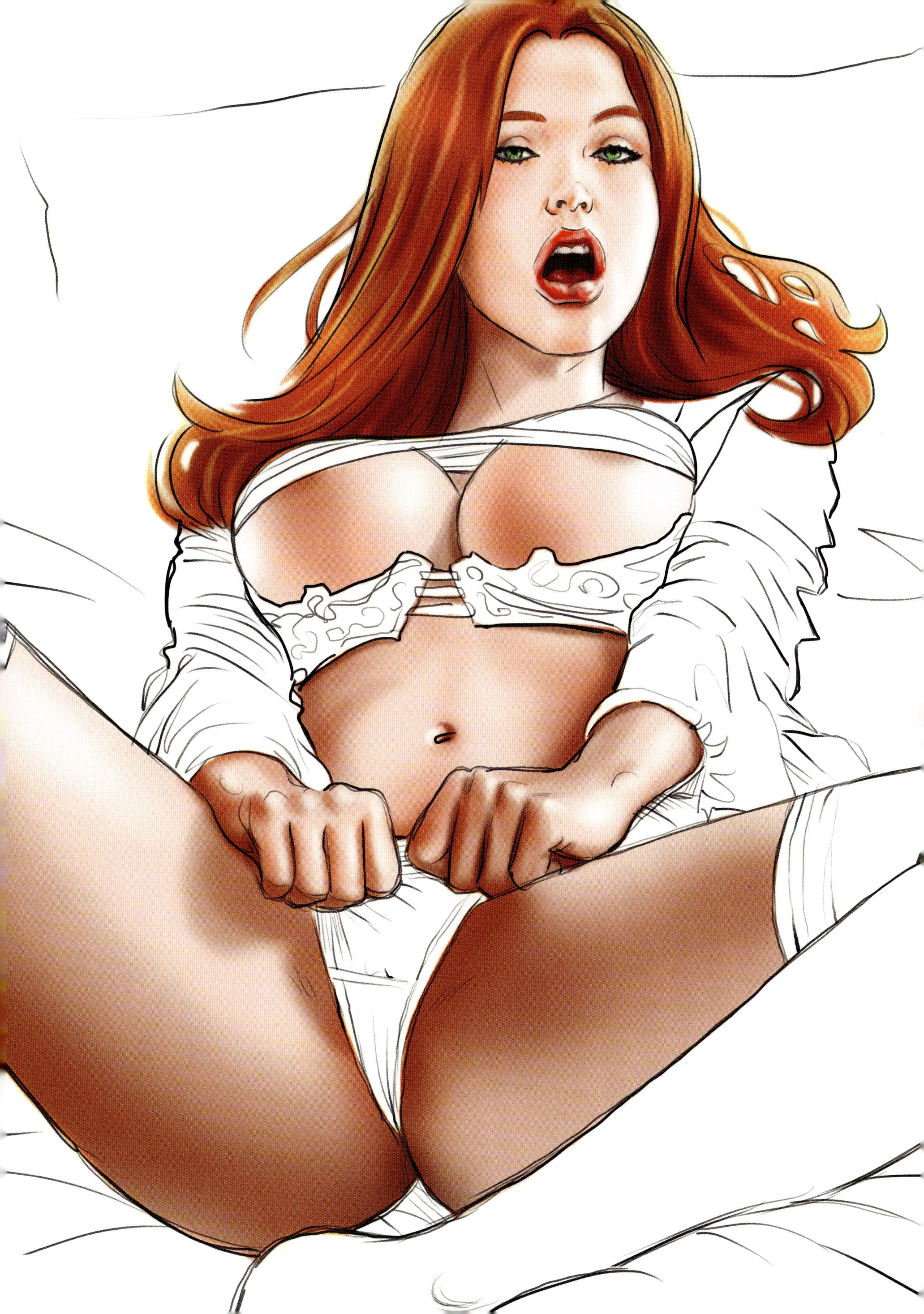

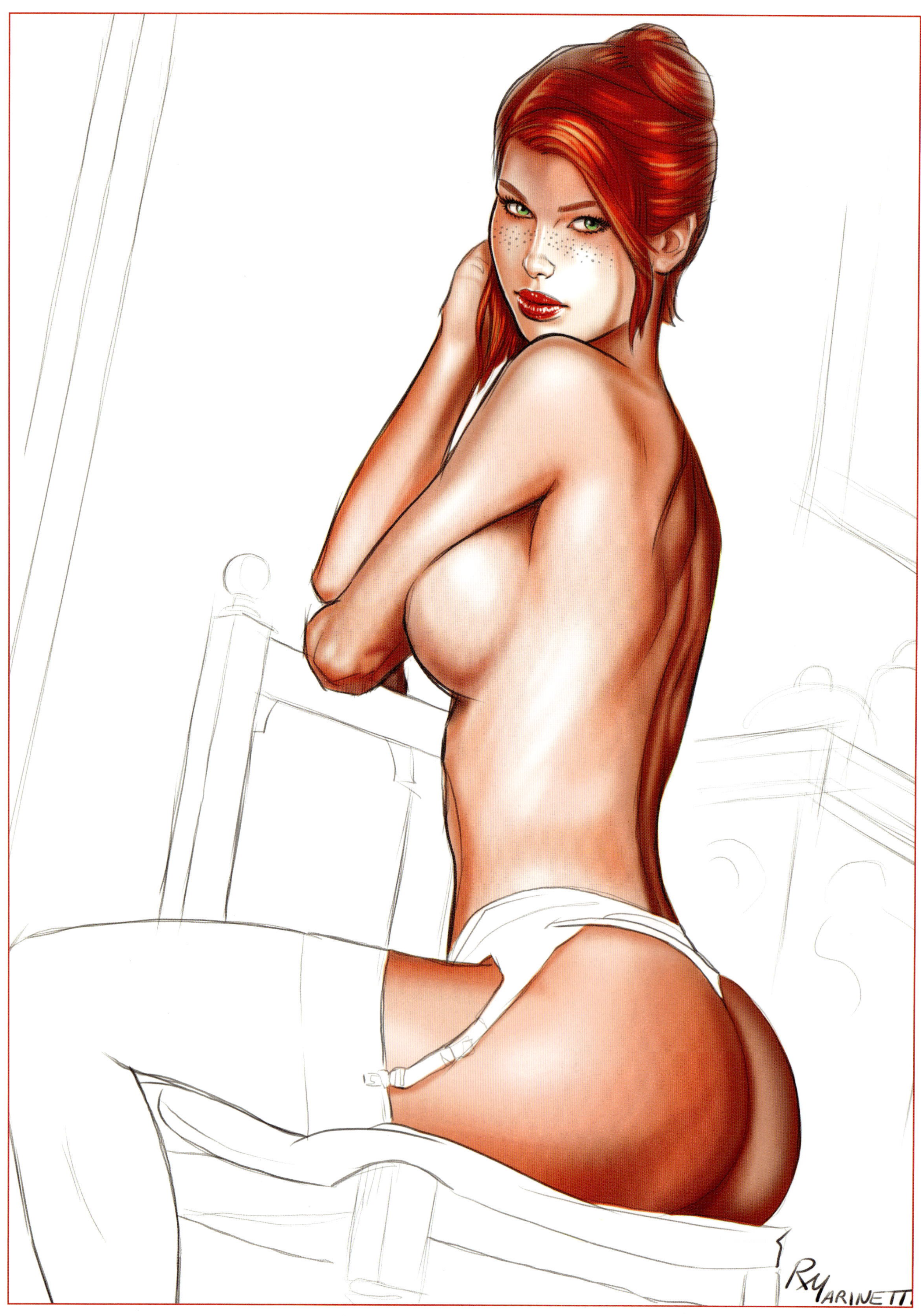
RM MARINETTI